CHELSEA GOLD

with love to
my son and daughter
Joel and Annie
to
Mike and Chezzy
and to
Sue
whose love and support made this book possible

CHELSEA GOLD

AWARD-WINNING GARDENS FROM THE CHELSEA FLOWER SHOW

JOHN MORELAND

CASSELLPAPERBACKS

above: this sophisticated contemporary garden was inspired by the life and times of the Roman poet Virgil; inscriptions from his poetry are featured throughout. Designed by Christopher Bradley-Hole, the Latin Garden won the ultimate accolade of the Best in Show Award.

First published in the United Kingdom in 2000 by Cassell & Co

This paperback edition first published in 2001 by
Cassell Paperbacks, Cassell & Co
Wellington House, 125 Strand
London WC2R 0BB

Distributed in the United States of America by Sterling Publishing Co., Inc.
387 Park Avenue South, New York, NY 10016-8810

A CIP catalogue record for this book is available from the British Library
ISBN 1841881260

Design Director **David Rowley**
Editorial Director **Susan Haynes**
Designer **Peter Butler**
Editor **Maggie Ramsay**
Printed in Italy by Printer Trento S.r.l

CONTENTS

INTRODUCTION

'...gardens should have a sense of theatre, if they are visually to stimulate and stir the emotions...'

The Royal Horticultural Society's Chelsea Flower Show is internationally famous throughout the gardening world and is generally regarded as the finest show of its kind. Among the many attractions, the outdoor show gardens have become a special favourite of both the media and the general public.

These gardens are created from nothing in just over two weeks, are on show for five days and are then destroyed! Within a week the area is returned to grass for the park of the Royal Hospital – until the show starts all over again the following year. It may sound like 'instant gardening' but this is far from the case. A Chelsea show garden takes many months of planning, sometimes up to two years. Those designers who regularly create gardens for Chelsea are starting to plan the next year's garden as soon as the show is over. They submit ideas just under a year ahead of the coming show and a special selection panel has the task of whittling down the many applications for the 25 or so available plots.

The show gardens are judged and each year a number are selected for the award of the much-coveted RHS Gold Medal. Although many people see the gardens when they visit the show, it seems a tragedy that these glorious creations have such a brief life. Fortunately, many of the sponsors and designers keep records of these award-winning gardens in the form of plans and beautiful photographs taken by some of the top photographers in the country. This book captures the magic of some of these gardens and gives an insight into how the designers were inspired to create such an extraordinary diversity of plantings and landscapes. Between 1989 and 1999 there have been 78 Gold Medal-winning gardens; I have selected those that most successfully seem to display the variety, innovation and inspiration that characterize the Chelsea Flower Show.

Stunning as all these gardens are, some are clearly rooted in practicality, whereas others go all out to capture an audience with their drama and wit. Indeed, gardens should have a sense of theatre, if they are visually to stimulate and stir the emotions, and this can be seen in all the great gardens, large or small throughout history. Consider the formal gardens of the grand French châteaux, created specifically as theatrical settings for masques and tableaux. The inspiration for these came from the extravagant gardens of the Italian Renaissance: the spectacular fountains and grottoes at the Ville d'Este, the 'water theatre' of the Villa Aldobrandini, among many others. The same gardens inspired the eccentric Englishman's 'follies': ruins, grottoes or temples placed in the landscape to surprise and delight the viewer. All use dramatic elements to create a unique sense of place. Gardens need not simply be about pathways, borders and lawns; rather, they should indulge fantasies and free the imagination…

opposite: Bunny Guinness's Writer's Garden is based around this tree house with its own moat, a tranquil retreat that would surely inspire any writer.

THE HERBALIST'S GARDEN

Not for her the traditional herb garden contained within neatly clipped box hedges and gravel pathways; the designer Bunny Guinness flips us into a mediaeval world of herbalists and fiery dragons, with edible, aromatic and healing herbs planted throughout the whole garden.

The site slopes up towards the back, and she exploits the changes in level to create two distinct areas, one overlooking the other. At the centre of the lower level is a baby dragon bathing in a round pool, watched by two enormous dragons – if roused, smoke billows from their nostrils. The dragons' heads were carved by the stonemason Mark Porter, who was responsible for all the stonework in the garden. Each head took him approximately two weeks to complete from a single block of Bath stone, weighing almost two tons. The heads arrived at the show on a large articulated lorry and had to be carefully craned into position.

From the dragons' heads a stone staircase curves away on either side, with the stony spines of the dragon running along the top of its rotund body. This follows the outer edge of the garden and is made up of great banks of chamomile, selected because it can be easily clipped into shape, and for its wonderful summertime aroma. A stone seat halfway up invites you to take your ease and savour the sweet-smelling air.

The steps are lined on the inner side with terracotta pots filled with many varieties of medicinal and culinary herbs. When you reach the upper level you will find a pleasant area with a backdrop of mixed woodland, ideal for alfresco dining or simply relaxing on a warm summer's day, taking in the scents rising up from the garden below.

Towards the rear of the lower level, within the curve of the staircases, is another sitting area, with two stone benches facing each other across a chequered pattern of stone slabs and cushioned squares of thyme. At the heart of this area a mediaeval arched doorway is framed by two fruit-laden citrus trees in terracotta pots. Beyond the timber doors lies the herbalist's retreat: a clever trompe l'oeil by the artist Martin Rodgers shows his inner sanctum, complete with pestle and mortar, hanging bunches of drying herbs, jars of remedies and his pet dragon!

The tremendous mixture of herbs is complemented by other herbaceous plants. Bright orange tulips and purple alliums are seen dancing above the softer tones of the scented drifts of lavender and santolina.

All too often, herbs are confined to a small area of the garden, with half a dozen or so varieties corralled within their clipped box hedge. How much more exciting to devote the whole garden to herbs planted not just for their culinary

above: the huge dragon's head provides a dramatic backdrop to the pom-poms of *Allium hollandicum* 'Purple Sensation', dancing above drifts of *Helichrysum italicum* and *Santolina rosmarinifolia*. Beyond, the old oak door stands half open, inviting you into the herbalist's inner sanctum...or, if you prefer, the garden shed!

opposite: a stone bench carved with mystic symbols is set amid aromatic banks of soothing chamomile, with a backdrop of *Viburnum opulus* 'Roseum' to add to the air of calm.

9

uses, but also for their aromatic or medicinal properties, or simply because they are attractive to look at. Such a garden would allow you to explore the vast number of herbal plants available, both wild and cultivated.

The growing of medicinal herbs goes back many thousands of years, to the early dynasties of China and the civilizations of the Middle East. The ancient Greeks and Romans amassed a large body of herbal knowledge, and although much of their written material was lost during the Dark Ages, monastic communities kept the traditions alive. In mediaeval times the crusaders reintroduced herbal knowledge from the East, and the monasteries did much to develop the medicinal use of herbs, side-by-side with culinary uses. Herbs stimulated the appetite and aided digestion: they also added to the flavour of food. With limited means of preserving food, herbs such as horseradish helped to disguise 'off' flavours – a number of herbs have now been found to have antibiotic properties, so they played an active role in food preservation.

The first 'physic', or healing, gardens were founded in Renaissance Italy, when knowledge ceased to be the sole preserve of religious communities, and was also sought by scholars and apothecaries. The Chelsea Physic Garden in London, established by the Society of Apothecaries in 1673, flourishes to this very day. Physic gardens played a major part in developing the knowledge of herbs. The famous 17th-century astrologer and physician Nicholas Culpeper listed more than 400 plants in his *Complete Herbal*, most of which were included for their medicinal uses.

In recent years there has been a revival in the practice of aromatherapy, which specifically uses the essential oils of herbs and other plants for their therapeutic properties. A form of aromatherapy was practised by the ancient Egyptians as long ago as 4500BC, and the Romans recorded their use of scented plant extracts for the sheer pleasure of perfumed baths and massage; the oil of chamomile was a great favourite. We now know that it contains azulene, a natural anti-inflammatory agent which helps to heal wounds and has a rejuvenating effect on skin; they fought against ageing every bit as much as we do today. So, not only does a garden full of herbs look wonderful, it could also be very good for your general wellbeing. A herb garden with a difference in every way.

above: lining the staircase, terracotta pots are generously filled with vibrant tulips and aromatic, culinary and medicinal herbs – *Mentha suaveolens* 'Variegata' in the foreground.
opposite: a patchwork of green, silver-grey and purple plants includes the purple castor oil plant (*Ricinus communis* 'Impala'), French lavender (*Lavandula stoechas*), chives, *Perilla frutescens* var. *crispa*, *Artemisia absinthium* and balls of box (*Buxus sempervirens*) and lavender (*Lavandula angustifolia* 'Hidcote').

Ajuga reptans 'Catlin's Giant' (bugle)
Alchemilla mollis (lady's mantle)
Allium hollandicum 'Purple Sensation'
Allium schoenoprasum (chives)
Aloe vera
Aloysia triphylla (lemon verbena)
Anethum graveolens (dill)
Angelica archangelica
Armeria maritima (sea thrift)
Armoracia rusticana 'Variegata' (variegated horseradish)
Arnica montana (leopard's bane)
Artemisia absinthium
Artemisia caucasica
Artemisia ludoviciana
Artemisia 'Powis Castle'
Bryonia dioica (bryony)
Buxus sempervirens (box)
Calendula officinalis 'Prolifera' (pot marigold)
Carum carvi (caraway)
Chamaemelum nobile 'Treneague' (chamomile)
Citrus (orange tree)
Cucurbita maxima (squash)
Cynara cardunculus Scolymus Group (globe artichoke)
Digitalis purpurea (foxglove)
Dryopteris affinis
Dryopteris filix-mas (male fern)
Equisetum arvense (mare's tail)
Eriobotrya japonica (loquat)
Erysimum cheiri (wallflower)
Erysimum hieraciifolium (Siberian wallflower)
Ficus carica (common fig)

Filipendula ulmaria 'Aurea' (meadowsweet)
Foeniculum vulgare 'Purpureum' (purple fennel)
Hedera helix (common ivy)
Helichrysum italicum (curry plant)
Heracleum sphondylium (cow parsley)
Humulus lupulus 'Aureus' (golden hop)
Hyssopus officinalis (hyssop)
Ilex aquifolium (holly)
Iris sibirica
Laurus nobilis (bay)
Lavandula angustifolia 'Hidcote'
Lavandula x *intermedia* (English lavender)
Lavandula stoechas (French lavender)
Levisticum officinale (lovage)
Lilium candidum (Madonna lily)
Lonicera japonica 'Halliana' (honeysuckle)
Luma chequen (myrtle)
Macleaya cordata
Melissa officinalis 'Aurea' (golden lemon balm)
Mentha spicata 'Crispa' (curly mint)
Mentha suaveolens 'Variegata' (apple mint)
Myrrhis odorata (sweet cicely)
Ocimum basilicum var. *purpurascens* (purple basil)
Origanum vulgare 'Aureum'
Pelargonium quercifolium (scented geranium)
Perilla frutescens var. *crispa*
Petroselinum crispum (parsley)

Plantago major 'Rubrifolia' (plantain)
Polemonium caeruleum (Jacob's ladder)
Primula veris (cowslip)
Primula vulgaris (primrose)
Prostanthera cuneata (mint bush)
Pulmonaria officinalis 'Sissinghurst White' (lungwort)
Ricinus communis 'Impala' (purple castor oil plant)
Rosa canina (dog rose)
Rosa 'Evelyn'
Rosa 'Phyllis Bide'
Rosmarinus officinalis 'Miss Jessopp's Upright' (rosemary)
Ruta graveolens 'Jackman's Blue' (rue)
Sagina subulata (pearlwort)
Salvia officinalis Purpurascens group (purple sage)
Santolina rosmarinifolia (cotton lavender)
Sempervivum tectorum (houseleek)
Tanacetum vulgare var. *crispum*
Tanacetum vulgare 'Silver Lace'
Taxus baccata (yew)
Teucrium x *lucidrys* (germander)
Thymus x *citriodorus* 'Aureus'
Thymus x *citriodorus* 'Silver Queen'
Thymus 'Porlock'
Thymus serpyllum 'Minimus'
Thymus vulgaris 'Silver Posie'
Tropaeolum majus 'Peach Melba'
Tulips
Viburnum opulus 'Roseum'
Viola odorata (sweet violet)
Viola tricolor (heartsease)

NEW ENGLAND COTTAGE

above: lilies are sure to be the first flowers to catch the eye at Mayflower cottage.

opposite: the brick path is edged with unclipped *Buxus* 'Green Velvet', interspersed with geraniums, violas, *Alchemilla mollis* and the pale spires of *Veronica gentianoides* 'Tissington White'.

Fiona Lawrenson has a great love of architecture, especially the architecture of New England, USA. A friend returning from a vacation in Nantucket brought her back a lavishly illustrated book, full of beautiful photographs of the houses so typical of the region. The neat, well cared for, yet slightly eccentric gardens caught her eye and sowed the seed of an idea – to recreate such a garden, complete with the house as the backdrop.

And here it is, a perfect reproduction of that New England style, with its beautifully weathered, lap-boarded front elevation and a roof of genuine cedar shingles, shipped in from the States; the American tiles are thicker than their European counterparts. The veranda, decked with scented climbing roses, makes an inviting link between house and garden. It looks cosy and welcoming, the perfect place to sit and watch the world go by. You can almost hear the creak of the old rocking chair on the well-worn boards and smell the warm, sweet aroma of mom's apple pie drifting out on the balmy air…

Fiona had noticed how the gardens – contained within their neat picket fences – are exquisitely traditional, but are more complex and original than they first appear. The planting is a charming and somewhat idiosyncratic mix of

above: the snowball flower heads of *Viburnum opulus* 'Roseum' and the globes of *Paeonia* 'Scarlett O'Hara' (foreground) and *P.* 'Buckeye Belle' pick up the colours of the white lilies and the deep pink *Lilium* 'Acapulco'.

opposite: set against a hedge of Western hemlock (*Tsuga heterophylla*), a rustic bench looks across the garden over a tub of the bright red *Pelargonium* 'Boogy'.

perennials, annuals, shrubs and roses. Its beauty lies in its spontaneity, whimsy and good old-fashioned no-nonsense approach. An example of this is the way the small bushes of box lining the main pathway have been left unclipped and are instead simply pinched out by hand, giving a much looser and softer look.

Few gardens rely quite so much on plants as a cottage garden. Being predominantly herbaceous, the skill lies in choosing plants that provide a continuous cycle of colour and fragrance throughout the spring and summer. Here, this is provided by such perennials as the early-flowering digitalis and dicentras and then the clumps of scented lilies such as *Lilium longiflorum*, *Lilium lancifolium* and *Lilium* 'Buff Pixie', the nicotianas and the perennial geraniums, *G. pratense* 'Mrs Kendall Clark', *G. clarkei* 'Kashmir White' and 'Kashmir Purple'. Then add to this the scents and colours of the abundantly flowering shrub roses, such as the reddish-purple *Rosa* 'Roseraie de l'Haÿ', offset by the apricot-buff of *Rosa* 'Buff Beauty'. Flowering shrubs can also, if chosen wisely, provide all-year-round interest. In this garden, as well as the evergreen box, there are bushes of blueberry, *Vaccinium corymbosum*, with its clusters of pale pink urn-shaped flowers, followed by berries with a blue bloom, sweet and edible. Even though some of the plants may look delicate, they are deceptively hardy and well suited to the extremes of the New England climate. As gardeners there say, 'If it'll grow in New England it'll grow 'most anywhere...'

The pathways running between the four square borders are made up of old red bricks laid in a mixture of herringbone and basket-weave patterns, with sanded joints. The main path leads from the front gate up to the veranda and the cross path, leading to a side gate, has at its opposite end a rustic bench set against a loosely clipped hedge of Western hemlock (*Tsuga heterophylla*).

The show garden got off to a near-disastrous start. The building of the façade had been the subject of a successful dummy run, away from the site. This was done to ensure that any major problems could be ironed out ahead of time and also to make sure that everyone knew exactly what they were doing. The building was then duly erected on the show site. But just before it was completed, a freak wind blew up from nowhere and the whole thing collapsed, falling forward, rather like a scene from a Buster Keaton film; unfortunately, in this case, two people were trapped beneath it. They were taken to hospital, but suffered no serious injury. Meanwhile, the façade was re-erected and the garden completed well on time.

Not only completed, but perfect in every detail, even down to the all-American mailbox from Boston. This arrived in a pristine state, so to give it its aged look it was battered and bashed, and given just the right touch of 'rusting' to make it seem a natural part of this timeless garden.

Tree and shrubs
Buxus 'Green Velvet'
Syringa vulgaris 'Andenken an Ludwig Späth'
Tsuga heterophylla
Vaccinium corymbosum
Viburnum opulus 'Roseum'

Herbaceous
Allium christophii
Aquilegia vulgaris
Centaurea major
Clematis viticella
Delphiniums
Dicentra spectabilis 'Alba'
Erysimum 'Bowles' Mauve'
Geranium clarkei 'Kashmir Purple', 'Kashmir White'
Geranium x *oxonianum*
Geranium pratense 'Mrs Kendall Clark'
Geranium sanguineum
Hosta 'Francee'
Hosta 'Frances Williams'
Heuchera micrantha 'Palace Purple'
Lilium 'Acapulco'
Lilium 'Buff Pixie'
Lilium lancifolium var. *splendens* (tiger lily)
Lilium longiflorum
Nepeta 'Six Hills Giant'
Paeonia 'Buckeye Belle'
Paeonia 'Scarlett O'Hara'
Pelargonium 'Boogy'
Phlox divaricata 'White Perfume'
Rosa 'Bobbie James'
Rosa 'Boule de Neige'
Rosa 'Buff Beauty'
Rosa gallica 'Versicolor'
Rosa 'Roseraie de l'Haÿ'
Veronica gentianoides 'Tissington White'
Viola cornuta 'Alba'
Viola 'Fiona Lawrenson'
Viola 'Molly Sanderson'

Annuals
Centaurea cyanus
Cosmos 'Sensation'
Nicotiana 'Lime Green'

GARDEN OF THE BOOK OF GOLD

An oasis of calm, created for His Highness Shaikh Zayed bin Sultan Al-Nahyan, President of the United Arab Emirates. His Highness, a deeply philosophical man, believes that horticulture transcends racial and religious barriers, and is thus the perfect vehicle for promoting peace throughout the world. The inspiration for this garden, designed by Charles Funke, came from an 18th-century poem about a prophet who sees, in the moonlight, an angel writing in a book of gold. Here, the book, in black granite with a gold leaf inscription, is inlaid on a single piece of white Carrara marble of breathtaking size: 3 x 2m (10 x 6.5ft). It is reflected in an 11.5m (38ft) long pool with a stepped surround of smooth white Portland stone. Stepping stones define the lower area, where the still surface of the water is brought to life by the water lily (*Nymphaea* 'René Gérard').

Surrounding the garden, 12 statuesque date palms (*Phoenix dactylifera*) provide an air of seclusion, magically filtering the sunlight through their gently waving fronds. The palm trees were carefully transplanted from the Shaikh's own garden in Abu Dhabi and prepared over many months prior to being flown to England a few weeks before the show. Filling in the gaps between the tall trunks of the palms are scented citrus trees (*Citrus sinensis)*, the windmill palm (*Trachycarpus fortunei*) and, at ground level, clumps of spiky grass (*Festuca gautieri*).

Set back under the shade of the trees are four hand-wire-worked arbours, providing a place to sit in quiet contemplation. This garden, very much in the eastern tradition, has elements that could be readily adopted in any setting.

THE OLIVE GROVE

above: terracotta pots filled with architectural plants such as this agave add a distinctly Mediterranean feeling to any garden, large or small.

They say the camera never lies, but when you look at these pictures it is hard to believe that it is not a hot summer's day in an old-established garden somewhere in southern France or Italy, on a hillside basking in that special Mediterranean sunlight. In fact, it is in the middle of London, in the middle of May, and the garden has been created in just over two weeks.

Two of the principal elements that help to create the illusion are, of course, the characteristic, pencil-thin, Italian cypresses (*Cupressus sempervirens*) and the wonderful olive trees (*Olea europaea*). The latter, with their gnarled and twisted trunks, give the impression that the garden is sited in an abandoned olive grove. Indeed, in re-creating an ancient olive grove, the designer, Mark Anthony Walker, wished to convey a sensation of great age. The sense of time is enhanced by the addition of 'later' garden elements such as stone walls, steps and water features cut into the hillside beneath the olives, suggesting the efforts of a nearby but unseen gardener.

The design was very organic: no fixed layout or planting plans were drawn up before the show, and much of the planting relied on informal decision-making during the building of the garden. The pattern of the pathways and the symmetry of the sunken courtyard are in deliberate contrast to the natural distribution of the stone walls and the olive and cypress trees above.

The garden is on a corner site and can be viewed along two sides. At one end you enter up a couple of rough-hewn stone steps to a pathway made up in traditional pebbling: fine pebbles are all laid in one direction to lead the eye forward. A thin line of stone acts as a retaining edge and beyond that on either side a soft line of lavender (*Lavandula multifida*) scents the air as you pass by.

Off to one side is an old terracotta olive jar lying forgotten on its side among the mixed planting of wild grasses, irises and red valerian (*Centranthus ruber*), a self-seeding hardy perennial that is very tolerant of dry conditions, making it ideally suited for an open, sunny site.

above: a huge olive jar lies abandoned amid an abundant mixed planting of wild and cultivated flowers and grasses.

The path leads on between the olive trees, which are underplanted with a mixture of sun-loving plants, including varieties of leptospermum, valued for their profusion of jewel-like flowers and aromatic leaves. Brighter colours here derive from the bright, saucer-shaped flowers of cosmos, its feathery leaves complementing the spiky foliage and scarlet blooms of the bottlebrush (*Callistemon citrinus* 'Splendens').

From the other side of the garden you can see where the path eventually leads down a number of broad stone steps into a small sunken area with a simple round pool as the central feature. Rough-cut, smooth-topped stone segments form the pool's edge; this is slightly overhung so as to create a shadow line, emphasizing the pattern at the bottom of the shallow pool of pieces of stone in various subtle tones. Around the pool is an intricate pattern of hand-laid pebbles, with narrow borders of young agapanthus extending around the base of the low dry-stone retaining wall that encloses the area.

Set into the wall is a small sandstone face of Neptune, made by Fiona Barratt. Neptune is spouting water and crowned by a splendid 'baby' cycas, commonly known as the Japanese sago palm. A host of sun-loving plants are set into and on top of the wall and backed with drifts of gypsophila, with varieties of osteospermum tumbling over the edge.

Throughout the garden you can spot individually decorated terracotta pots made by the ceramic artist Jane Hogben; some have been left unfilled, to stand

opposite: a profusion of sun-loving Mediterranean-style plants help to give this garden its unique sense of place.

Climbing plants
Actinidia deliciosa
Rosa 'Cécile Brünner'

Shrubs
Abutilon vitifolium 'Tennant's White'
Acca (Feijoa) sellowiana
Callistemon citrinus 'Splendens'
Ceanothus griseus 'Yankee Point'
Chamaerops excelsa
Choisya ternata 'Sundance'
Cistus x *corbariensis*
Cistus x *pulverulentus* 'Sunset'
Cistus x *purpureus*
Cycas revoluta
Elaeagnus x *ebbingei*
Fremontodendron californicum
Halimium umbellatum
Lavandula angustifolia 'Hidcote'
Lavandula multifida
Leptospermum sp.
Metrosideros excelsus
Olearia macrodonta
Perovskia 'Blue Spire'
Phormium tenax purpureum
Pinus sylvestris
Pittosporum tobira 'Nanum'
Pittosporum tobira 'Variegatum'
Rosmarinus officinalis sp.

Ruscus aculeatus
Teucrium fruticans 'Azureum'
Wisteria sinensis 'Alba'

Perennials and wall plants
Acanthus spinosus
Achillea filipendulina 'Gold Plate'
Agapanthus africanus
Agave americana
Armeria maritima 'Corsica'
Ballota pseudodictamnus
Clematis florida 'Sieboldii'
Dianthus 'Garland'
Echinops bannaticus 'Taplow Blue'
Echium fastuosum
Euphorbia myrsinites
Euphorbia polychroma
Euphorbia robbiae
Euphorbia characias subsp. *wulfenii*
Gentiana verna
Geranium macrorrhizum
   'Ingerwersen's Variety'
Gypsophila paniculata
Helianthemum 'Ben Fhada'
Helianthemum 'Red Dragon'
Helianthemum 'Wisley Primrose'
Iris sibirica
Lathyrus latifolius 'White Pearl'
Nepeta x *faassenii*

Rhodiola rosea
Salvia x *sylvestris* 'Lye End'

Summer flowers
Helichrysum petiolare
Pelargonium (various varieties)
Osteospermum (various varieties)

Wild flowers
Adonis aestivalis (pheasant's eye)
Borago officinalis (borage)
Centranthus ruber (red valerian)
Chrysanthemum segetum (corn marigold)
Echium vulgare (viper's bugloss)
Glaucium flavum (horned poppy)
Helianthemum nummularium
Lupinus arboreus (tree lupin)
Origanum vulgare (marjoram)
Papaver rhoeas (field poppy)
Silene uniflora (sea campion)
Verbascum thapsus (verbascum)
Verbena officinalis (vervain)

Grasses
Ammophila arenaria (marram grass)
Briza media (quaking grass)
Festuca glauca (blue fescue)
Lagurus ovatus (hare's tail)

as pieces in their own right, others have been planted up with a variety of plants, including large standard clipped bay trees, cycas and agaves. But undoubtedly the stars of the piece are the beautiful specimen 'standards' of *Wisteria sinensis* 'Alba' with their great drooping racemes of scented white flowers.

Although this style of garden is typical of warmer climes around the world, it is surprising how many of these plants are tolerant of more temperate zones. Even the olive tree, so much a part of the Mediterranean scene, can be grown in colder regions if near the coast, where the climate tends to be milder and free from heavy frosts. Those plants that are susceptible to low winter temperatures can be kept in their pots, plunged in the ground during the summer months and then taken into a conservatory or greenhouse to overwinter.

Above all, this garden demonstrates how it is possible to create a particular sense of place – somewhere that looks and feels very special – through clever selection of the right materials in combination with the right plant varieties, particularly the scene-setting olive trees, Italian cypresses and wisteria.

above: *Clematis florida* 'Sieboldii' tumbles down next to a small cycas in a patterned terracotta pot.
right: crowned by a flourishing cycas, Neptune spouts water into a border of *Iris sibirica*, *Agapanthus africanus* and *Lavandula angustifolia* 'Hidcote'.
opposite: two beautiful white standard wisteria complete the impression of a garden in the sunny Mediterranean.

THE LOCK-KEEPER'S GARDEN

above: *Primula vialli, Lobelia* 'Fan Scharlach' and the red-tinged *Ligularia dentata* 'Desdemona' flourish beside the small stream.
opposite: the 'canalside' setting shows how a typical cottage garden can merge seamlessly into a waterside planting.

The inspiration for this garden came when the designer Peter Hogan was walking out with his family one summer's evening, along the towpath of a stretch of the Basingstoke canal. His attention was caught by a number of old barges painted in the distinctive, highly decorative and colourful style known as 'castle and roses'; the barges were lying up alongside a lock-keeper's canalside cottage. The scene gave Peter the idea of designing a variation on the theme of the cottage garden, which would evoke nostalgia for the days when horse-drawn barges transported their great loads the length and breadth of the country, along the national network of canals.

There is just a glimpse of the barge at the rear of the garden alongside the beautifully reconstructed cottage. This type of cottage, with its curved roof, is unique to the Stratford canal; the tradition of the rounded roof arises from the fact that the builders used the same timber framework that formed the curves in the construction of the canal bridges. The cottage would make a perfect potting shed or garage in another garden in the present time, while the 'house-boat' could provide the focus for a wonderful children's adventure play area.

The whole garden was constructed by students of Pershore College of Horticulture in Worcestershire, under the direction of Frank Hardy, Vice Principal of the college. His planting design called for the establishment of a variety of different planting within the site. To one side of the cottage is a small vegetable plot, with its line of scarlet-flowered runner beans standing proudly

above lettuces, beetroot and herbs. In front, a great profusion of colour tumbles down a series of 'terraces' planted in typical cottage garden style. The striking group of red and yellow lupins picks up the vibrant colours of the 'castle and roses' palette: the yellow lupins are called 'Deborah Woodfield'; the scarlet ones are, appropriately, called 'Chelsea Pensioner'.

A footpath from the cottage runs down one side of the garden across a sturdy timber bridge set above the 'overspill stream' from the canal. The introduction of water allows for the added attraction of moisture-loving plants in a cottage garden setting. Bright kingcup marigolds (*Caltha palustris*) appear early in the year, along with drifts of primulas, including the very distinctive *Primula vialii*, with its violet and red-tipped head. The bold foliage of the ligularias makes a strong statement, the reddish-purple-tinged *Ligularia dentata* 'Desdemona' contrasting with the light green *Ligularia* 'Gregynog Gold'.

Throughout the rest of the garden, a generous mixture of flowering shrub and herbaceous planting provides all-year-round interest. The shrub border merges into a backdrop of semi-mature trees, including the paper-bark maple (*Acer griseum*), weeping birch (*Betula pendula*) and common alder (*Alnus glutinosa*).

The sponsor of the garden, the *Sunday Express*, invited the British Waterways Board to attend the press day review. So delighted were they, that they aranged for an 'extended family' of bargees to come along in their traditional costumes, bringing samples of their hand-decorated 'castle and roses' utensils.

Bog garden

Astilbe 'Etna'

Astilbe x *arendsii* Weisse Gloria

Caltha palustris 'Flore Pleno'

Houttuynia cordata 'Chameleon'

Iris pseudacorus 'Variegata'

Iris sibirica

Ligularia dentata 'Desdemona'

Ligularia 'Gregynog Gold'

Ligularia przewalskii

Lobelia 'Fan Scharlach'

Mimulus aurantiacus

Primula carniolica

Primula denticulata 'Rubra'

Primula vialii

Rheum palmatum
    'Atrosanguineum'

Rodgersia pinnata

Trollius 'Alabaster'

27

THE NATIONAL TRUST CENTENARY GARDEN

above: the central water feature consists of a narrow rill and three bubble fountain slabs, each smaller than the other, giving a false sense of perspective. The clean, modern lines of the water feature present a quiet contrast to the classic herbaceous borders, full to abundance on either side.
opposite: *Cytisus* 'Boskoop Ruby' and *Iris* 'Solid Mahogany' make a startling splash of colour beneath the variegated leaves of *Pittosporum tenuifolium* 'Variegata'.

The National Trust wished to celebrate its one hundredth birthday in a show garden, to be sponsored by the *Daily Telegraph*. Clearly the garden had to reflect not only Britain's heritage but also the quality that is the hallmark of this respected trustee of some of the country's most beautiful gardens.

To this end, designer Arabella Lennox-Boyd decided that the garden would have classic English herbaceous borders, in the tradition of many of the Trust's most famous gardens, such as Hidcote Manor in Gloucestershire, and Sissinghurst in Kent. But she would also give it a contemporary spin with the jet black painted pergolas and a central water feature of polished black Cumbrian slate.

The garden is laid out on a long rectangle, measuring approximately 10m (32ft) wide by 22m (70ft) long. The plan is a simple cruciform with a strong central axis; the cross paths lead off to left and right under the white wisteria hanging from the pergolas. The garden can either be viewed as self-contained, or in the context of a much larger one in the traditional style.

The backdrop is provided by a silver birch woodland, underplanted with masses of viburnum and osmanthus. These create dark pools of shade, making

above: the dark yew and copper beech act as a perfect backdrop to a classic herbaceous border. Masses of white roses and perennials are chosen for their varied forms: *Iris* 'Avanelle'; *Lilium longiflorum*; *Rosa* 'Iceberg' and *Rosa* 'White Meidiland'; *Lupinus* 'Noble Maiden'; and sweet rocket (*Hesperis matronalis* var. *albiflora*). The border is spiced up by the red leaves of the beetroot 'Bull's Blood' and the tall stands of *Atriplex hortensis* var. *rubra*.

it hard to tell exactly where the garden ends. The woodland is set behind a dry-stone wall of Cumbrian slate. The stone for this was selected from an old, tumbled-down section of wall from the Burlington quarries at Kirkby-in-Furness, the quarries that supplied all of the slate for the garden. Two clipped yews frame the opening in the wall, which leads to a mown pathway running off into the woodland beyond. Just to one side of the path is a classic urn, which is positioned precisely on the central axis to provide a focal point to the garden.

The water feature reinforces this central axis and consists of a narrow, slate-lined rill linking three squares of slate, each just a little bit smaller than the other, receding, to give a false sense of perspective. The idea of a formalized stream can be traced back to the Persian 'paradise' gardens and from there to the symmetrical water features around the palaces and tombs of the Mogul emperors of India. This style of water feature was later adopted by garden designers in the early 20th century; Edwin Lutyens, for example, used it in some of the country house gardens he designed with Gertrude Jekyll.

There is a reservoir and pump under the slabs of slate, providing a bubble fountain for each one. The slate squares are very slightly dished, to ensure that the water is held before it cascades along the full length of all four sides; if the slabs were flat the water would travel the shortest distance to trickle over the four quarters only!

It is the wonderful herbaceous borders that bring the whole garden to life with their subtle abundance of texture and colour. Eight magnificent yews reinforce the symmetry and give an overall sense of stability. This is further enhanced by the framework of shrubs, the fresh green of the pittosporum and variegation of the cornus contrasting with the deep purple of the cotinus and copper beech hedge. These themes are picked up by the herbaceous planting. The spiky green clumps of the variegated hostas and grasses contrast with the stands of red orach and white foxgloves, the burgundy reds of the miniature dahlias and *Cytisus* 'Boskoop Ruby', the rich deep purple of the *Iris* 'Sable' and the smoky-pink blush of the poppy *Papaver orientale* 'Patty's Plum'. The colours at the red end of the spectrum can be difficult to use as the eye is immediately drawn to them, foreshortening the distance. Here they are toned down by the variegated leaves: the greys of santolina and *Artemisia* 'Powis Castle' and the grey-green, jagged leaves of the cardoons.

The whole border is highlighted by the sparkling white of the roses, irises and sweet rocket, and the erect exclamations of the white lupins. Above it all, rise the misty clouds of the flowering *Crambe cordifolia* and heady scent of the masses of Bermuda lilies (*Lilium longiflorum*).

Mixed herbaceous

Abutilon vitifolium var. *album*
Ajuga reptans 'Atropurpurea'
Ajuga reptans 'Braunherz'
Alchemilla mollis
Allium karataviense
Allium multibulbosum
Anthemis punctata subsp. *cupaniana*
Aquilegia 'Darkest Purple'
Artemisia absinthium 'Lambrook Silver'
Artemisia 'Powis Castle'
Asplenium scolopendrium
Athyrium filix-femina
Atriplex hortensis var. *rubra*
Beetroot 'Bull's Blood'
Berberis thunbergii 'Atropurpurea Nana'
Brachyglottis 'Sunshine'
Camassia leichtlinii 'Alba'
Centaurea 'Black Ball'
Cistus x *loretii*
Clematis 'Duchess of Edinburgh'
Convolvulus cneorum
Cornus alba 'Elegantissima'
Cornus stolonifera
Cotinus coggygria 'Royal Purple'

Crambe cordifolia
Cynara cardunculus
Cytisus 'Boskoop Ruby'
Dahlia 'Bednall Beauty'
Dianthus 'Dainty'
Dianthus 'Dewdrop'
Dianthus 'Fusilier'
Dicentra spectabilis 'Alba'
Digitalis purpurea f. *albiflora*
Dryopteris filix-mas
Elymus magellanicus
Euphorbia dulcis 'Chameleon'
Euphorbia griffithii 'Dixter'
Euphorbia mellifera
Euphorbia palustris
Euphorbia polychroma
Foeniculum vulgare 'Smokey'
Fuchsia splendens
Geranium sylvaticum 'Album'
Hebe subalpina
Hesperis matronalis var. *albiflora*
Heuchera micrantha 'Palace Purple'
Heuchera 'Pewter Moon'
Hosta 'Thomas Hogg'
Hosta ventricosa
Incarvillea delavayi alba

Iris 'Avanelle'
Iris 'Caliente'
Iris 'Sable'
Iris 'Solid Mahogany'
Iris 'White Swirl'
Lilium longiflorum
Lilium martagon var. *album*
Lobelia 'Queen Victoria'
Lupinus 'Noble Maiden'
Matteuccia struthiopteris
Miscanthus sinensis 'Variegatus'
Nectaroscordum siculum subsp. *bulgaricum*
Nepeta racemosa 'Snowflake'
Papaver orientale 'Blue Moon'
Papaver orientale 'Patty's Plum'
Penstemon digitalis 'Husker Red'
Pittosporum tenuifolium
Pittosporum tenuifolium 'Variegata'
Plantago major 'Rubrifolia'
Polemonium caeruleum var. *album*
Polygonatum x *hybridum*
Potentilla 'Gibson's Scarlet'
Rosa 'Grand Hotel'
Rosa 'Iceberg'
Rosa 'Lilli Marlene'
Rosa 'Sander's White Rambler'

Rosa 'Seagull'
Rosa 'White Meidiland'
Salvia officinalis Purpurascens Group
Santolina serratifolia
Sedum ruprechtii
Silybum marianum
Spiraea nipponica 'Snowmound'
Stachys byzantina 'Cotton Boll'
Stachys byzantina 'Silver Carpet'
Stephanandra incisa 'Crispa'
Taxus baccata
Viburnum tinus 'Eve Price'
Viola 'Bowles' Black'
Viola 'Mrs Lancaster'
Viola 'Mollie Sanderson'
Viola 'Scarlet'
Viola 'White Pearl'
Viola cucullata albiflora
Viola riviniana Purpurea Group

Hedge; woodland; pergolas

Betula pendula
Fagus sylvatica Purpurea Group
Osmanthus ilicifolius
Viburnum opulus
Wisteria floribunda 'Alba'

As with so many of the show gardens, there was an eleventh-hour crisis; in fact in this case there were two. It had been agreed that the Trust would supply the large stone urn that was to be *the* focal point. Somewhere along the line there had been a breakdown in communications – no urn! Runners were dispatched to scour the local antique stores. A Luton van duly turned up and out stepped a veritable mountain of a man, 6ft-plus of rippling muscle. He walked to the back of the van, embraced the urn, picked it up and started to stride the length of the garden. The site stopped, jaws dropped. His companion trotted behind with the lid. The appointed place was reached and the urn duly positioned. He turned round, gave everyone a glorious smile, walked back to the van and drove away. Universal gasps. Jaws closed and, as one, everyone moved towards the urn. It was then that they discovered it was made of fibreglass!

The garden was all but completed. Last-minute watering was being carried out and Mike Chewter, who has built many a Chelsea show garden, had switched on the pumps to check that all was well with the water feature. First, strange little white patches appeared on the jet black paintwork of the pergolas where they had been splashed from the watering. Then someone noticed a creamy white scale growing out from the centre of the slate slabs. General consternation…what was happening? It was the London water! Everyone got down on to their hands and knees to gently scour the offending scale. A neutralizing liquid was added to the water and all was well again – just in time for the judges.

opposite: a classic herbaceous planting, including *Lupinus* 'Noble Maiden' and the rare *Incarvillea delavayi alba*, with the variegated leaves of *Hosta* 'Thomas Hogg' and *Miscanthus sinensis* 'Variegatus'. Peeping out beneath the purple-bronze leaves of *Euphorbia dulcis* 'Chameleon' is a red pansy (*Viola* 'Scarlet').
below: the hot reds of the miniature *Dahlia* 'Bednall Beauty' and *Cytisus* 'Boskoop Ruby' are toned down by the silver-grey foliage of *Convolvulus cneorum* and the variegated leaves of *Pittosporum tenuifolium* 'Variegata'.

A GARDEN FOR ROSES

above: a variety of foliage plants – silvery *Artemisia* 'Powis Castle', heart-shaped *Epimedium* x *rubrum* and tightly curled parsley – provide a foil to the striking white plumes of *Astilbe* 'Bressingham Beauty' and the vivid flowers of yellow *Rosa* 'Korresia', crimson *Rosa* 'Marjorie Fair' and pink *Rosa* 'Ballerina' rambling in from above.

opposite: the garden's changing levels draw the eye upwards through a riot of colour. In the foreground, the patio rose 'Pretty Polly' flourishes in a terracotta pot.

This garden unashamedly celebrates the glories of the English rose in all its many forms. In particular, it highlights one special bush hybrid tea rose, the fragrant, vibrantly scarlet 'Spirit of Youth', established by rose grower Robert Wharton. This rose was being shown for the first time and named in honour of the Prince's Youth Business Trust, with all profits from future sales going to support the work of the Trust founded by the Prince of Wales to help young people to set up in business.

Floribunda, hybrid tea, low-growing ground cover roses, splendid climbers and ramblers, patio roses and 'old-fashioned' shrub roses are beautifully blended with a mix of perennial herbaceous plants, such as gypsophila, astilbe, artemisia, tiarella, iris, hosta, geum and geranium. And for all-year-round interest David Stevens has designed the garden against a background structure of shrubs and delicate foliage trees: rhododendron, azalea, spiraea, bamboo, acers, cercidiphyllum and silver birch, with the creamy pink heads of the woodland foxglove providing delicate highlights.

Two of the rhododendrons used are very large, being over 45 years old. Known as Bill and Ben, they have become something of a good luck talisman as David has used them in many of his gold medal gardens. On this occasion one

right: the hot, rich colours of rhododendrons 'Purple Splendour' and Windlesham Scarlet', the deep red ground cover *Rosa* 'Marjorie Fair' and the coppery leaves of *Acer palmatum* 'Bloodgood' and *Acer palmatum dissectum atropurpureum* are kept in check by the many white highlights: *Rosa* 'Iceberg', marguerite daisies, *Astilbe* 'Snowdrift' and *Hydrangea petiolaris* peeping over the wall.

of them was particularly attractive to a pair of blackbirds who decided to make a nest and lay three eggs during the build-up and show period. After the show the plant in question had to be very carefully loaded – with mother blackbird in place – and returned to the nursery where the eggs were duly hatched!

Such a garden does not – apart from the exceptional circumstances of the Chelsea Flower Show – establish itself in a single season, but with the inclusion of planted terracotta pots, colour and foliage can be introduced before the garden reaches its height of abundance.

The terrace at the front of the garden is constructed of the time-honoured traditional paving materials of random York stone and brick. Central to the terrace is the round raised bed filled with a single rose variety, the dazzling 'Spirit of Youth', and dotted around with splashes of white: nicotiana, marguerite daisies and astilbes.

Curving around the central bed on one side is a still pool with a spout of water discharging from a terracotta lion mask set on the face of the brick

retaining wall at the rear. Simple groups of water irises are placed around the pool to break up the hard edge of the paved surround.

On the other side of the terrace, wide steps lead up beneath a series of dark stained timber pergolas, bedecked with the fragrant and delicate pink blooms of the climbing rose, *Rosa* 'New Dawn'.

Directly ahead beyond the first landing and rising up on low timber stilts, a beautifully crafted open-sided summerhouse in the Lutyens style is made from old bricks, distressed timber and pegged clay roof tiles. Turning to the right, a further flight of steps takes you up to a semi-circular paved area with a simple white cast-iron and timber seat. Behind the seat, echoing the semi-circle, a series of iron hoops held between tapering timber posts provides the perfect framework for climbing roses, a treatment often used by the Victorians.

A final flight of narrow steps takes you up to the summerhouse, nestling among great banks of rhododendrons – an ideal vantage point from where you can fully savour the sight of the roses and the scent-laden air.

above: the size of the plot is similar to many suburban gardens. To give a greater sense of space the garden is worked across the diagonal at 45°, this being the longest line in any given square, and can work equally well – as in this case – with a rectangle.

A MODERN ROOF GARDEN

above: specially made domes, planted with aromatic evergreens, reflect the shape of the skylights. The flowers of the *Achillea* bring a touch of stardust to the lunar-style landscape.

For a number of years the designer Dan Pearson lived in a flat with its own roof garden, at the top of a three-storey building in Vauxhall, in the centre of London. The creation of the garden we see here drew from his personal experience. He felt very strongly that he should accept the open, exposed environment of a roof garden and not attempt to disguise it or change it in any way, for example by using such devices as screens and trellises. Accordingly all the plants are drought-resistant and coastal varieties; all are able to withstand the high level of exposure to wind and light. With no intrusions from neighbouring gardens, Dan also felt it necessary to accept and work with the powerful presence of the open sky. Indeed, this inspired the concept of a lunar-style landscape, with mounds of planting echoing the hemispheres of the perspex skylights.

This bold, uncompromising approach to the exposed nature of roof gardens is also seen in the work of a number of other international designers. Topher Delaney, one of America's most inventive landscape architects, introduced a series of freestanding, colourful wind socks into her design for a large roof garden in San Francisco; they give the garden the overall appearance of a piece of kinetic art as they flutter and sweep round at the command of the prevailing winds. The South American artist and designer, the late Roberto Burle Marx, also created some extraordinary 'open' roof gardens in both Rio de Janeiro and Sao Paulo: great swirling patterns made up of materials of various colours and textures, such as coloured gravels, interspersed with areas of planting, so that when you look down on the garden it appears as a huge canvas, an abstract work of art.

In Dan Pearson's garden, the conservatory, with its serpentine glazed front, provides an all-weather garden room and affords a view across the whole roof and the surrounding vistas. The lighting pendants follow the curved form, illuminating a line of Mexican golden barrel cacti (*Echinocactus grusonii*), each in its own 'long tom' terracotta pot. The cacti may be placed outside in summer, but require protection during the colder months. The lead-covered aerofoil roof profile, representing an aircraft wing, overhangs the building, providing a degree of shade in the summer months. A staircase rises within, and the floor of the

below: an unusual, somewhat eerie palette of colours in this planting comes from violet-tinged *Euphorbia dulcis* 'Chameleon', purple sage, bronze fennel and French lavender, in conjunction with the silvery-grey foliage of *Verbascum* 'Helen Johnson', cotton lavender (*Santolina chamaecyparissus*) and the curry plant (*Helichrysum italicum*).

the open, treeless, grassy prairies of North America suggested the planting of a mixture of grasses in the exposed rooftop environment. French lavender continues the spiky theme of the grasses, while the Iceland poppies seem to occur at random, as if they were wild poppies in a meadow.

conservatory is a mixture of decking and gravel, giving the effect of extending the outside area into the interior space.

A plain timber deck provides a pleasant outdoor sitting space, which is furnished with a pair of modern chaises longues designed by Dan's brother, Luke Pearson. With a framework of powder-coated aluminium, they are upholstered in an all-weather permeable material – used by the Army – which permits water to pass through without it becoming sodden. This means they can be left outside in rain, frost or snow, without fear of damage, an important bonus for a roof garden, where out of sight is sometimes out of mind.

At the centre of the seating area, a round glass-topped table reflects the sky. Its shape is echoed by the large, wide, frostproof terracotta pot, full to the rim with a carpet of *Echeveria elegans*, a stemless succulent which grows as a silvery-blue rosette of fleshy leaves with antenna-like pink flowers. At the sides, large, powder-coated aluminium containers display the striking, creamy-white bark of multi-stemmed Himalayan birch (*Betula utilis* var. *jacquemontii*), underplanted with a mixture of thrift (*Armeria maritima*) and the blue-green grass, *Festuca glauca*. Multi-stemmed trees were chosen as they tend to be shorter and are more stable in the event of high winds. The fact that they are growing in the restricted space of a container can also slow down their rate of growth. The thrift and festuca combination is also carried the full length of the bed running down one side of the garden.

Elsewhere, drifts of different grasses have been planted to catch the movement of light breezes; the burnished coppery hair-like leaves of the New Zealand hair sedge (*Carex comans* 'Frosted Curls') complement the loosely tufted, pale brown, evergreen leaves of *Carex testacea*. The erect stems of the teasels stride among the clumps of grasses, along with the distinctive spires of *Verbascum* 'Helen Johnson'. This verbascum's coppery-orange flower heads pick up the striking colour of the Iceland poppies (*Papaver nudicaule*); seemingly scattered at random, the poppies give the impression of having self-seeded at will.

Interspersed among the general planting are the specially constructed 'domes', measuring approximately 1m (3ft) across and 0.5m (20 inches) high. These are planted with four varieties selected for their all-year-round interest and fragrant foliage: two sweet-smelling evergreen thymes – *Thymus* 'Silver Posie', with bright golden foliage, and the silvery, variegated *Thymus* 'Bertram Anderson' – the curry plant (*Helichrysum italicum*), and cotton lavender (*Santolina chamaecyparissus*), both with aromatic, silver-grey leaves.

The garden cleverly combines an air of contemporary sophistication with a feeling of natural harmony. It is clearly an ideal place to relax and enjoy the sun, to entertain friends or simply to get away from it all, far from the madding crowds below.

Tree
Betula utilis var. *jacquemontii* (Himalayan birch)

Perennials
Achillea sp.
Armeria maritima (thrift)
Astelia chathamica
Chamaemelum nobile (chamomile)
Cynara cardunculus (cardoon)

Dipsacus fullonum (teasel)
Echeveria elegans
Echinocactus grusonii (golden barrel cactus)
Euphorbia dulcis 'Chameleon'
Foeniculum vulgare 'Purpureum' (bronze fennel)
Helichrysum italicum (curry plant)
Lavandula stoechas subsp. *pedunculata* (French lavender)

Papaver nudicaule (Iceland poppy)
Salvia argentea
Salvia officinalis Purpurascens Group (purple sage)
Santolina chamaecyparissus (cotton lavender)
Thymus x *citriodorus* 'Aureus'
Thymus x *citriodorus* 'Bertram Anderson'
Thymus serpyllum 'Lemon Curd'

Thymus 'Silver Posie'
Verbascum 'Helen Johnson'

Grasses
Carex flagellifera
Carex comans 'Frosted Curls'
Carex testacea
Festuca glauca

THE ZENECA GARDEN

above: suggestive of the
mediaeval alchemist's art, the
garden juxtaposes mysterious,
magical purples and blues with a
mass of varied, vibrant green
foliage, bursting with life.

This glorious garden, designed by Nuala Hancock and Mathew Bell, takes us
into the world of alchemy, full of mystical symbolism and references to the elemental themes of earth, water, air and fire. The timeless pursuit of knowledge,
medicine and science lies at the heart of the Zeneca garden, whose professed
message is that of bringing ideas to life.

The shape of the site determined the dominant form of the ellipse – suggesting the elliptical orbit of the planetary bodies. The design is essentially that
of a mediaeval herb garden, with low quartered beds surrounding a central
pool and layers of tall enclosing planting rising up beyond the linking pathways.
However, the innovative use of materials such as slate, glass and iron give a contemporary impression, which is further reinforced by the intensity of the
planting, with its rich palette of colour and strong rhythmic form. Blue is the
dominant note, in association with deep purple, violet and magenta, with highlights of pale gold and silver.

A major clue to the garden's identity is to be found in the mosaic keystone
set at the front entrance. Here is the sign of Zeneca, the letter 'Z', which was
the mediaeval alchemist's symbol, meaning 'to solve'. Around the mosaic is the
inscription 'As above, so below'. Alchemy, it is said, is the rainbow that attempts

to link the earthly and heavenly planes. This theme is picked up at the head of the garden, at its highest point or zenith, where an ornamental wrought-iron centrepiece supports aloft three richly coloured stained glass panels that form a rainbow of light linking earth and sky. The scenes within the stained glass are of the elemental themes of water, earth, air and fire. Across the panels, a dove soars skyward and returns to earth, symbolizing the cyclical alchemical process whereby solids are changed into liquid form, then re-materialized.

The idea for these images was drawn from an 18th-century French manuscript which carried the inscription 'If you dissolve the fixed and make fixed the volatile and make fast the winged thing, it will make you live in safety.' Alchemists throughout the ages have believed that, given the right astrological configurations, base metals such as lead might be turned into gold that would in turn become an elixir of life, with its promise of immortality…

From beneath the highest point there flows a cascade of water – the 'fountain of life', symbolizing the cleansing panacea, or 'cure all' – into a shimmering pool, the heart of the garden. In the pool, set on a square pane of glass, a composition of coloured glass spheres and apothecary jars filled with coloured waters acts as a focal point of ethereal light and colour. The theme of healing,

above: glass – used for the stained glass panels, coloured spheres and apothecary jars, and the clear pane upon which they stand – may seem an unlikely garden material, but it corresponds to the alchemist's fascination with opposites: it is fragile yet durable.

43

flowing water is echoed in the undulating forms of the wrought-iron railings that enclose the garden.

Another piece of ancient alchemical wisdom holds that it is in the understanding of the correspondence between fundamental opposites – such as Earth and Sky, Sun and Moon, Night and Day, Male and Female, Matter and Spirit – that perfect health and longevity can be achieved. In this garden are many expressions of such opposites.

The pathways are of rectangular tiles of blue-green slate. Integrated into this are two large round cobblestone mosaics by the mosaic artist Maggie Howarth. These depict the seven-pointed alchemical Sun and Moon and are set at opposite ends of the long ellipse. The mosaics provide platforms for the garden seats, the 'solar' and 'lunar' thrones, which face each other across the central pool in solemn conversation. The thrones were made by the designer Ray McNeill, who delights in recycling old lengths of timber to create unique pieces of furniture and objets d'art.

Throughout the garden the wonderful array of plants creates a dramatic effect by the inspired combinations of colour and form. Indeed, in certain areas, the planting appears to have a quality of shimmering iridescence, symbolically suggestive of both mediaeval alchemy and contemporary science. The extraordinary intensity of the *Allium* 'Purple Sensation' and the sparky globes of *Allium christophii* seem almost to carry an electric charge; the blue-violet flames of French lavender glint among the smoky foliage of bronze fennel; the lobed, spiny leaves of the Scotch thistle (*Onopordum acanthium*) erupt from mixed beds; the cool, silver-blue lights of *Elaeagnus commutata* and the glittery filigree of *Salix exigua* are set against the glow of lime-green euphorbia and the sulphur-yellow flowers of rue. Running through the whole garden, creating perfect harmony and representing the most obvious subject of all for an alchemist's garden, is *Alchemilla mollis*, its felted leaves bedecked with beads of dew, like liquid mercury.

This is the sort of garden that would be the delight of anyone who enjoys experimenting and wishes to be bold and courageous in their planting. It also demonstrates how it is possible to integrate the skills of many different artists and craftsmen – the blacksmith, the potter, the mosaicist, the furniture maker, the stained glass artist – to create a garden that is quite unique.

above: the bold globes of *Allium hollandicum* 'Purple Sensation' are bound to catch the eye. Supporting them are the feathery leaves of purple fennel, the flame-like tufts of French lavender (*Lavandula stoechas* subsp. *pedunculata*), the warm pink glow of *Lychnis viscaria* 'Splendens' and the lime-green bracts of *Euphorbia amygdaloides* var. *robbiae*.
below: *Iris* 'Royal Touch' and (in the foreground) purple sage reinforce the purple colour scheme.
opposite: 'orbs' of clipped bay stand on either side of the throne.

A TOUCH OF PARADISE

Bringing a taste of the tropics to Chelsea, this garden is filled to abundance with exotic plants that, despite their delicate appearance, can also thrive in a more temperate zone providing some care is taken.

At the heart of the garden the designer Bunny Guinness has created a Caribbean-style 'weekend shack' set upon stilts, with its own decked veranda overlooking the lily pool. The shack has a framework of whitewashed poles and its grass thatched roof is tied in at the ridge with hemp rope. The walls are timber lap-boards stained a pale forget-me-not blue, while the shutters are the deep cobalt blue of tropical skies. Leading away from the shack and running around one side of the pool is the timber boardwalk with its 'balustrade' of tensioned hemp rope and whitewashed posts, each with a sea-urchin 'cap'.

Elsewhere in the garden the pathways are made of cut log sections set into beach sand – with a generous scattering of seashells to add authenticity.

But above all, it is the exotic planting that creates the illusion of being in a tropical paradise, especially the fresh, green, sail-like leaves of the Japanese banana (*Musa basjoo*). Some of the sub-tropical palms are surprisingly hardy and will lend their striking architectural forms to gardens in temperate zones as long as they are given a sheltered, sunny spot. Two spectacular examples are the Canary palm (*Phoenix canariensis*), with its great spray of spiky fronds, and the Chusan palm (*Trachycarpus fortunei*), sometimes referred to as the windmill palm because of its spread of large, fan-like, deeply divided leaves. The cordylines (*Cordyline australis*) are also fairly hardy; they are often mistaken for palms, but are in fact members of the agave family and are commonly known as New Zealand *cabbage* palm, just to confuse matters further.

One especially exotic feature is the grass tree (*Xanthorrhoea australis*), often referred to as 'Captain Cook's blackboy': legend has it that the honourable Captain mistook a group of them for advancing figures on the beach. The grass tree is a long-lived perennial, with a short, stout trunk, a round 'head' and a spray of silvery-green leaves from which extends a tall, thin, candle-like flower, some 60cm (2ft) high. This gives the overall impression of some extraordinary headdress…hence the Captain's case of mistaken identity. This, like some of the

below: the rich lilac-blue of *Hydrangea macrophylla* is picked up by the *Lobelia* 'Cascade Blue'. Next to the hydrangea, the crown imperial (*Fritillaria imperialis*) produces an unusual-looking head of orange flowers. A canna in the background provides another flash of orange.

other more tender plants, will not tolerate frost, but if grown in a pot it could be plunged into the ground during the summer and then brought inside for the colder months of the year.

There are many other architectural plants, such as the two *Xanthosoma violaceum*, with their great, arrow-shaped leaves, on either side of the veranda, and the bright yellow-flowered arum lily (*Zantedeschia elliottiana*). Spiky clumps of *Phormium* 'Yellow Wave' are set beneath the young Canary palm and against the yellow-mottled leaves of *Abutilon pictum* 'Thompsonii', which bears yellow-orange flowers. A cluster of nasturtiums form a mat of colour beneath the palm tree.

Around the edge of the footpath, a number of moisture-loving perennials grow in the margins of the pool. These include astilbes, rodgersia and *Ligularia dentata* 'Desdemona', with its large, purple-bronze, heart-shaped leaves and deep orange flowers. The garden is also studded with terracotta and cobalt blue glazed pots containing sprays of light green ferns and lilac-blue hydrangeas.

To complete the effect of a garden of paradise, Bunny Guinness has included the exotic-looking *Lotus berthelotii*, with its clusters of rich, scarlet, claw-like flowers and silver foliage. The trumpet-like, heavily fragrant blooms of the Bermuda lily (*Lilium longiflorum*) form a cool contrast to the fiery orange flowers and purple-green leaves of the cannas.

Certainly, in this garden, you could easily imagine yourself on a Caribbean island, sitting in the cool shade of your veranda and sipping a cool rum punch with the sunny sound of 'steel pans' playing in the distance…not to mention the chattering of monkeys…

above: a jungle pathway of wood 'slices' set in sand, lined on either side with dense planting. Beneath the spiky leaves of *Astelia chathamica* 'Silver Spear' and *Yucca elephantipes*, scarlet pelargoniums tangle with daisies (*Erigeron karvinskianus*) and blue marguerites (*Felicia amelloides*). The golden trumpets of datura (*Brugmansia aurea*) hang down over the terracotta pot.
opposite: the boardwalk that leads to the shack takes you past a miniature date palm under-planted with orange-red nasturtiums (*Tropaeolum majus* 'Red Wonder'). Behind these, the swordlike *Phormium* 'Yellow Wave' contrasts with the giant, rhubarb-like leaves of *Gunnera manicata*.

Trees and shrubs
Abutilon pictum 'Thompsonii'
Brugmansia aurea
Chamaerops humilis (dwarf fan palm)
Cordyline australis
Cycas revoluta (Japanese sago palm)
Fatsia japonica
Melianthus major
Musa basjoo (banana)
Phoenix canariensis (Canary palm)
Phoenix roebelenii (miniature date palm)
Trachycarpus fortunei (windmill palm)
Xanthorrhoea australis (grass tree)
Yucca aloifolia, Y. elephantipes, Y. filamentosa, Y. gloriosa 'Variegata'

Perennials
Agapanthus praecox subsp. *orientalis*
Agave americana 'Variegata'
Arundo donax 'Variegata' (giant reed)
Astelia chathamica 'Silver Spear'
Canna indica
Cynara cardunculus (cardoon)
Erigeron karvinskianus
Felicia amelloides (blue marguerite)
Hydrangea macrophylla
Lotus berthelotii

Pelargonium sp.
Phormium 'Yellow Wave'
Phyllostachys aurea (golden bamboo)
Rheum palmatum 'Atrosanguineum'
Verbena 'Red Cascade'
Zantedeschia elliottiana

Moisture-loving perennials
Cyperus papyrus
Gunnera manicata
Hosta sieboldiana var. *elegans*
Ligularia dentata 'Desdemona'
Mimulus 'Firedragon'
Rodgersia pinnata 'Superba'
Xanthosoma violaceum
Zantedeschia aethiopica 'Crowborough'

Bulbs
Fritillaria imperialis 'Rubra'
Lilium longiflorum (Bermuda lily)

Annuals
Convolvulus tricolor 'Blue Flash'
Lobelia 'Cascade Blue'
Nicotiana sylvestris
Ricinus communis (castor oil plant)
Tropaeolum majus 'Red Wonder'

CLASSICAL CALM WITH A TOUCH OF TOMORROW

above: a bed of arum lilies provides a calm central feature of the formal garden. In the corner a wrought-iron gate – incorporating a design of arum lilies – leads through to the secret haven of the woodland garden.

opposite: around the lawn, the borders are filled with a truly glorious abundance of herbaceous planting.

This walled town garden creates a mood of comfort and beauty, and provides a refuge from the stresses of city life. It is intended to be lived in rather than simply to serve as a spectacle for special occasions, and to be a constant source of inspiration and joy for the enthusiastic plant lover. Although for the most part designed on classical lines, the bold use of traditional materials such as terracotta, wrought iron and Portland stone introduces a contemporary note.

The designer Xa Tollemache had a married couple in mind. He is a successful businessman with conventional taste and simple demands of his garden. He needs a place where he can entertain his friends and clients and where everything is just right as he walks out onto the terrace. She, on the other hand, is more Bohemian, a child of the sixties, who seeks a wild area, a secret haven where she can retreat with a good book and commune with nature. And here is the solution: two distinct gardens – formal and informal – in one.

We enter the formal area across a terrace of York stone; although random in size, the paving slabs are all rectangular and laid to form a neat patchwork. On

above: a pleasingly simple blue and white colour scheme in the woodland garden: silver birch, white foxgloves and blue poppies (*Meconopsis betonicifolia*).

Wall plants

Actinidia deliciosa 'Tomuri'
Clematis 'Betty Corning'
Clematis x *durandii*
Clematis x *eriostemon* 'Hendersonii'
Clematis 'Niobe'
Clematis 'Prince Charles'
Clematis 'Etoile Rose'
Exochorda x *macrantha* 'The Bride'
Parthenocissus henryana
Rosa 'Albéric Barbier, *R.* 'Goldfinch',
  R. 'Sander's White Rambler',
  R. 'Seagull', *R.* 'Wedding Day'

Herbaceous borders

Acanthus spinosus
Allium hollandicum 'Purple Sensation'
Allium christophii
Anchusa azurea 'Loddon Royalist'
Artemisia absinthium 'Lambrook Mist'
Artemisia ludoviciana 'Valerie Finnis'
Campanula persicifolia 'Chettle Charm'
Campanula persicifolia 'Wortham Belle'
Cistus 'Elma'
Cistus ladanifer
Cistus ladanifer var. *sulcatus*
Cistus x *verguinii*
Crambe cordifolia
Cynara cardunculus
Dianthus 'Mrs Sinkins'

Digitalis x *mertonensis*
Erigeron karvinskianus
Foeniculum vulgare 'Purpureum'
Geranium clarkei 'Kashmir White'
Geranium 'Johnson's Blue'
Geranium nodosum
Geranium pratense 'Mrs Kendall Clark'
Geranium renardii
Geranium sylvaticum 'Album'
Geranium sylvaticum 'Mayflower'
Hesperis matronalis var. *albiflora*
Iris 'Deep Black'
Iris 'Harriette Halloway'
Lavandula x *intermedia*
Lavandula pinnata
Mysotis sp.
Nepeta x *faassenii*
Nepeta racemosa 'Walker's Low'
Rosa gallica 'Versicolor', *R.* 'Heritage',
  R. 'Kent', *R.* 'Reine des Violettes',
  R. 'Tuscany Superb', *R.* 'William
  Lobb'
Salvia nemorosa 'Lubecca'
Salvia x *sylvestris* 'Mainacht'
Scabiosa lucida
Trifolium repens 'Purpurascens'
Verbascum chaixii 'Gainsborough'
Verbascum chaixii 'Mont Blanc'
Veronica gentianoides
Viola riviniana Purpurea Group

either side of the terrace are eight tapering brick columns set in two squares. These were inspired by the multitude of brick chimneys that rise up from the designer's own home, Helmingham Hall in Suffolk. Indeed, the columns were hand made by the original brick makers, the Bulmar Brick & Tile Company, with brickyards dating back to 1450. The columns are linked at the top by a simple open cupola form in black wrought iron. Two large, elegant, terracotta urns herald the entrance to the lawn. Made by the potter Rupert Blamire, they are very much of our time but undoubtedly inspired by classical styles.

The garden is enclosed by walls made up of bricks rescued from a derelict farmhouse, softened by an abundance of climbers and deep perennial borders in every imaginable shade of pink and purple, with old favourites such as roses, lavender, catmint and clematis growing alongside some of the newer varieties of campanula, artemisia, euphorbia and the electric *Allium christophii*. An especially striking combination of colour and form comes from the juxtaposition of *Allium hollandicum* 'Purple Sensation' and the *Iris* 'Deep Black'. Along the south-facing wall is a cordon-trained *Exochorda* x *macrantha* 'The Bride' in its luscious green summer dress, having shed its spectacular racemes of large white flowers earlier in the season. *Crambe cordifolia*, with its mass of delicate white flowers, now rises cloud-like above the border; other white highlights come from *Dianthus* 'Mrs Sinkins' and *Verbascum chaixii* 'Mont Blanc'.

At the centre of the lawn there is a formal box-edged bed echoing the shape of the brick-edged lawn and filled with a mass of white arum lilies (*Zantedeschia aethiopica* 'Crowborough'). The distinctive shape of the lily flower provides the dominant motif for the wrought-iron panels set into the garden wall and the wrought-iron gate leading through into the wild garden. The ironwork was manufactured by the artist-blacksmith John Churchill; as with so many of these gardens, the designer has enlisted the talent of other artists to provide some of the special features. The lawn ends with a curving line of five young lime trees (*Tilia* x *euchlora*), with a mixed planting of trees beyond the garden wall to further enhance the sense of enclosure.

A hint of whimsy is introduced into the formal garden by an 'armchair' set amid the herbaceous border; a large stone slab forms the seat and square-clipped box hedging the back and arms.

Passing through the gate into the secluded woodland garden, we cross a narrow, slow-running stream. To one side, at the centre of the informal pool, is a water feature made from a half-ton block of roughly hewn Portland stone by

below: although the two gardens – separated by a brick wall – are very different, they share common elements: York stone paving, a simple stone bench seat, and several of the same plants appear in both gardens.

the contemporary sculptor Louise Gardener. Water flows continuously from a hole at the top, yet without making any ripples to disturb the surface of the pool; you hear only the gentle sound of the water falling over the face of the stone – a sound often chosen to assist relaxation.

A path of randomly placed York stone slabs set in gravel spirals in front of an ancient Irish stone bench set into the edge of the woodland, which wraps around the end of the garden behind the wall. Along the path's edge is a blend of natural herbaceous woodland planting. Drifts of perennial geraniums (*G. sylvaticum* 'Album' and 'Mayflower', which also appear in the herbaceous borders of the formal garden) run between the bold cut forms of the hellebores and the bleeding hearts of the dicentra. The serene spires of white foxgloves (*Digitalis purpurea* f. *albiflora*) and the sky blue of the acid-loving Himalayan blue poppy

(*Meconopsis betonicifolia*) stand out against a backdrop of mixed shrubs. The wine-coloured leaves of *Cotinus* 'Grace' blend with the purple to bronze of the elders (*Sambucus nigra* 'Guincho Purple') and the greyish-purple leaves of *Rosa glauca*, with highlights from the white flowers of the viburnums and spiraeas.

The pathway returns to the terrace past a curving, tumbled-down section of walling that maintains the privacy of the informal garden and displays a selection of terracotta pots by Alexander Macdonald Buchanan. The pots are filled with a wonderful profusion of plants, including two making their debut here, both in pastel colours: the pale yellow *Petunia* 'Prism Yellow' and the soft pink *Nemesia* 'Melanie'.

Like a happily married couple, this garden has two distinct identities – but with many aspects in common – living side by side in perfect harmony.

above: a stone seat, edged with clipped box, is set amid verbascums, *Campanula persicifolia* 'Chettle Charm', *Salvia* x *sylvestris* 'Mainacht', *Rosa gallica* 'Versicolor' and alliums.
top left: the base of the woodland seat is softened with the daisy-like flowers of *Erigeron karvinskianus* and delicate forget-me-nots.
left: this exhilarating massed planting includes catmint, *Dianthus* 'Mrs Sinkins', anchusa, cardoons, alliums, bronze fennel, and double-flowered campanulas.

A JAPANESE TEA GARDEN

above: a *tsukubai*, the stone basin traditionally used for washing hands before the tea ceremony, flanked by the bold foliage of *Hosta* 'Invincible' and *Hosta undulata* var. *univittata*, and the spiky leaves of the dwarf bamboo.
opposite: the tea house – or garden pavilion – is reached by two stone slabs forming a simple, off-set bridge over the pool. Beside the waterfall stands the very distinctive 'cloud-pruned' Japanese holly (*Ilex crenata*).

There is little doubt that traditional Japanese gardens, at their highest level, are among the most sublime of all gardens. This is largely due to their underlying expression of the deeply philosophical religion of Buddhism; nowhere is this seen more clearly than in the tea garden. All too often in the West, gardens created in the Japanese style are totally lacking in any understanding of the fundamental Buddhist principles. Here, however, we have a rare example of how it is possible to interpret the symbolic combination of rocks, water and plants, and in the process to create a truly beautiful garden in a Western setting. To achieve this, designer Julian Dowle joined forces with his professional colleague and friend Koji Ninomiya, one of Japan's leading exponents of the art of gardening.

Although we in the West may not fully understand every nuance, we can gain an insight into the philosophy of Buddhism by absorbing the overall tranquillity of the Japanese garden. It is designed in such a way that we are drawn into feeling relaxed and in harmony with nature.

The tea garden, or *roji*, is the setting for the age-old Buddhist tea ceremony. The Grand Masters teach that before beginning the ceremony one should attain a state of contentment, '*Chisoku anbun* ... One learns to be content, and only then does one make a fire, bring water, boil it and prepare tea by one's own labour. The tea thus prepared is offered to the Buddha, then to guests, and finally partaken of oneself.' The host of a tea gathering will water the garden and wash clean the pathway over which his guests will pass. In these simple acts he is also 'cleaning' his mind, 'discarding all feelings of prejudice and evil passions.' The guest, too, must cleanse his hands and mouth at the stone basin, the *tsukubai*. At that moment, his mind is said to be in a state of '*Shinshin kore rojo* ... where both body and soul are clean and free from any stain.' This act of washing has obvious parallels with the symbolic purification by Holy Water in the Christian church.

Rocks have a strongly symbolic role in many Japanese gardens. In the tea garden they are seen as the 'core', the origin of life and water. Even though they may be situated within a town, tea gardens are often perceived as being set in the mountains, within the lush bamboo and pine forests. Such is the case here, where the planting is very bold and simple, and rises up behind the tea house.

In the middle distance a waterfall runs down from the mountainside and spills gently into the pebbled, still pool in the foreground. Across the pool two

slabs form an off-set stone bridge; myth has it that the devil is a simple fellow and can only run in straight lines. It is hoped, therefore, that if you are being chased by him, he will run straight over the bridge and fall into the water and drown! A gravel path encircles the pool and leads up into the forest. At the point where it goes out of sight, Koji placed a small boulder tied up with black twine. This is known as *Tomeishi* and is an implicit sign that you cannot go beyond. It was there for the benefit of the judges, requesting that they go no further.

No expense was spared to re-create the impression of the forested slopes so typical of the inner mountainous regions of Japan. But due to the distance and complex plant disease regulations, the plants could not come from Japan direct, so many were brought in from nurseries in Italy. On the left-hand side of the garden there are great banks of the bamboo *Phyllostachys aurea*, which give a visual link to the other varieties of bamboo that run up through the woodland planting, especially the black-stemmed *Phyllostachys nigra*.

A few very special trees were shipped in from the Netherlands to give a distinctively Japanese appearance and create the illusion of maturity around the waterfall. First there is the Japanese five-needle pine (*Pinus parviflora*) which, because of the sharpness of its needles, is often planted near the entrance of a garden to ward off evil spirits. It is also traditional to have one of its branches hanging down low over the footpath so that the visitor is obliged to bend to pass beneath it, so performing a gesture of humbleness. The beautiful Japanese maple, *Acer palmatum dissectum atropurpureum*, has deeply cut, rich purple leaves. Most striking of all is the tiny leaved Japanese holly (*Ilex crenata*); 'cloud pruned' on an S-shaped trunk, it manages to combine the delicacy of a bonsai tree with a sense of stability, like a tree that has grown forever on this particular mountainside. Each of these specimens is between 30 and 40 years old. Overall the three cost in the region of £6,000 which, although it included shipping them across to the site, was nonetheless a big lump out of the budget. Fortunately a visitor to the show saw them, fell in love with them and bought the lot! They are now happily growing somewhere in a Japanese garden in the rolling green landscape of the Cotswolds.

For the most part, the colour palette throughout the garden plays on the many subtle variations of the green foliage, ranging from the lighter variegations of the hostas and bamboos through to the dark needles of the conifers. In contrast to the greens are the rich, dark clarets of the Japanese maples.

In the whole of the garden there is but one flower, the *Iris sibirica* planted at the water's edge. And quite extraordinarily, there was literally only one flower in bloom at any one time...as one died so another would open.

Because the areas that can be easily inhabited are so limited, much of Japan is very crowded and the space available for gardens is precious. Amid the frenetic lifestyle of the Japanese cities, gardens provide a much-valued sanctuary to replenish the mind and soul. As the world generally seems to be becoming more hectic, maybe we all need such a sanctuary.

below: a delicate latticed bamboo gate stands at the entrance to the garden.

THE REFLECTIVE GARDEN

above: an elegant canvas canopy echoes the form of the arum lilies.

opposite: simple sawn York stone steps direct the eye from the abundant herbaceous border to the reflective stillness of the canal.

An urban or roof-top garden that explores the combination of modern architectural forms with traditionally inspired planting. The designer Michael Balston wished it both to reflect the past and also to look towards the future as we enter the new millennium.

On one side of the garden, flying canopies of canvas, detailed by the engineers Buro Happold, are held aloft by hi-tech, thin steel masts and cross booms, reminiscent of the great sails of the old tall ships. These are reflected in the clear shallow waters of the canal, running parallel to a deck of stained timber, laid at an oblique angle. The angle is picked up by the narrow lines of the sawn York stone steps that divide the lawn into three. The steps emerge from deep shrub borders and end at neat triangular beds of arum lilies sitting in the canal and acting as punctuation marks. The rectangular shape of the plot is transformed by these dynamic diagonals, yet the garden retains an overall sense of tranquillity with the stillness of the canal.

The garden's focal point is a shining, faceted wall of stainless steel on a raised platform of sawn York stone. At the centre, held high by arching steel columns, a flower-shaped canopy, echoing the forms of the arum lilies and the nearby gunnera, is designed to act as a sunshade, rainwater collector and energy-generating solar panel. Accumulated rainwater is directed into the main canal and energy from the solar panel provides power for garden lighting.

The principal planting area, filled with trees, shrubs and mixed herbaceous plants, wraps around the stainless steel wall. The planting is deep and chosen for textural effect and colour. The large mass of the purple-leaved *Acer palmatum* 'Bloodgood' is the perfect foil for the silver foliage of *Artemisia ludoviciana* and the spiky, metallic lilac-purple of *Allium christophii*. Throughout there is a broad mix of shrubs, including cercis, viburnum, photinia, rhododendrons, and the bold architectural forms of phormiums, yuccas and *Chamaerops humilis*. To complement these the herbaceous planting includes crambe, geraniums, irises, peonies, primulas and euphorbias, with a selection of ferns and grasses.

With its time-honoured blend of traditional planting to offset a vision of the future, this garden achieved the ultimate accolade of the Best in Show Award.

A GARDEN OF GOLDEN MEMORIES

This garden, designed for the charity Help the Aged, is full of warm golden colours; a garden in which to relax and reminisce, to walk or sit quietly in peace and tranquillity.

Although he had the elderly in mind, the designer Robin Williams feels it is too simplistic to create 'a' garden for 'the' elderly, as though you could satisfy every need. Older people have very varied needs: some are as fit as people half their age, while others have genuine disabilities that have to be taken into account. This garden could be seen as a communal garden, which could be shared and possibly maintained by others.

The focal point of the garden is the water feature: a radiant sun fountain discharging into an enclosed still pool and glimpsed through a Chinese-style moon-gate or, in this case, a moon-window. This is beautifully constructed with concentric circles of brick, the inner ring being made up entirely of tapering 'specials' to avoid the sight of ugly splayed joints.

In order to ensure that the water does not simply trickle over in a narrow stream at the lowest part of the moon-window, a plate of clear glass has been positioned on the front face of the brickwork, forming a miniature 'weir', which gives a wider and fuller appearance to the waterfall as it comes though the opening. Both the fountain and the waterfall introduce a note of natural vitality into the garden, along with the soothing sound of gently falling water.

To one side of the water feature is the imposing Gothic-style conservatory that allows the garden to be enjoyed throughout the year. In the cooler months it is a light, airy retreat, the glass providing protection and making the most of the sun's rays. The rear section of the conservatory is glazed with mirrors; this not only obscures the wall but also gives a greater illusion of space within. When it is warmer outside, with doors and windows opened, the conservatory is a summer dining room, perfect for meals that could easily extend out onto the surrounding wide paved terrace.

above: a simple plan with the open area of the lawn before the main water feature and a perimeter path providing easy access to every part of the garden.

above: Claude, the terracotta cat, caught in the act of pawing at a butterfly.

opposite: soft white and yellow plants make a garden feel more spacious; they also suggest springtime, a season of optimism, energy and contentment. A few touches of yellow's complementary colour, violet, bring harmony to the overall scheme.

For easy access there is a generous pathway of random stone paving, with a contrasting brick edge, running around the perimeter of the garden. Along the way there are simple white-painted bench seats, positioned to give different views and experiences of the garden. One is under the shade of a tree by the sundial, looking across the open prospect of the garden to the moon-window and the conservatory beyond. Another is in the sheltered, planted-up corner beside the water feature, allowing one to enjoy both the sounds of the water and the fragrances of the planting.

Throughout the garden, the predominant colour of the planting ranges across the yellow spectrum, from glowing golds to the softer pastel shades, offset by uplifting touches of blue, violet and white.

In the larger pool, we see reflections of the rich yellow flag iris (*Iris pseudacorus*) framed by the moon-window bedecked in floating white clouds of the climbing rose, *Rosa* 'Seagull'. Beds on either side of the smaller pool are filled with the variegated leaves of *Cornus alba* 'Elegantissima', great clumps of the sulphur-yellow *Verbascum* 'Gainsborough' and groups of the warm apricot-yellow hybrid musk *Rosa* 'Buff Beauty', with the translucent violet-blue petals of the bearded iris 'Jane Phillips' floating through the planting. Elsewhere in the garden, fragrant masses of the cream-coloured *Rosa* 'Tynwald' mingle with the bushy clusters of the golden *Euonymus fortunei* 'Emerald'n'Gold'. The trees also pick up the colour theme: the leaves of *Acer platanoides* 'Drummondii' are broadly edged with creamy white, and those of *Sambucus racemosa* 'Plumosa Aurea' are golden-yellow.

In this garden the lawn, the green sward, is all important. There is something very calming and reassuring about a well-maintained lawn. The fact that it is looked after regularly can provide routine and a sense of continuity for many elderly people.

There is one mischievous note in this idyllic haven of tranquillity: a delightfully crafted terracotta cat called Claude, balancing precariously on one of the brick piers, can be seen reaching down to paw at an unsuspecting clay butterfly that has just alighted. Designed by Robin, both Claude and the butterfly were modelled by the potter Christopher Hemstock. This simple touch characterizes the overall appeal of a warm, welcoming garden with a magical timeless quality.

Mixed borders

Acer platanoides 'Drummondii'
Athyrium felix-femina
Aucuba japonica 'Crotonifolia'
Campanula poscharskyana 'Stella'
Cornus alba 'Elegantissima'
Carex oshimensis 'Evergold'
Cotinus coggygria
Euonymus fortunei 'Emerald'n'Gold'
Euonymus fortunei 'Variegatus'
Genista hispanica
Hosta 'Thomas Hogg'
Hypericum 'Hidcote'
Iris pseudacorus
Iris sibirica
Iris 'Olympic Torch'
Lavandula angustifolia 'Hidcote'

Lupinus 'Chandelier'
Phormium tenax Purpureum Group
Rhus typhina 'Laciniata'
Sambucus nigra 'Guincho Purple'
Sambucus racemosa 'Plumosa Aurea'
Santolina chamaecyparissus var. *nana*
Solanum crispum
Verbascum chaixii 'Gainsborough'
Wisteria sinensis
Wisteria venusta

Roses

Rosa 'Buff Beauty'
Rosa 'Golden Jubilee'
Rosa 'Perle d'Or'
Rosa 'Seagull'
Rosa 'Tynwald'

A FOREST GARDEN

above: the log cabin is a typical feature of the Finnish countryside – in fact it is the genuine article, shipped over from Finland. *Verbascum* 'Gainsborough' and *Iris* 'Amber Queen' bring a touch of sunlight to the planting.
opposite: bright yellow *Geum* 'Georgenburg', deep blue *Ajuga reptans* 'Catlin's Giant' and the paler blue tubular flowers of *Corydalis flexuosa* 'Père David' are dominant amid a profusion of other species beside the grassy pathway.

This garden is an extraordinary achievement and demonstrates the extent to which a designer will go to achieve authenticity in every detail. The designer in question is Julie Toll and she was working in conjunction with the trade organization Pro-Carton, who wished to demonstrate their genuine commitment to sustainable forestry in the production of paper and carton board for packaging. The intention was to re-create a typical piece of Scandinavian pine and spruce forest and to show how a wild garden could be incorporated within such a setting.

In order to get a feeling for the woodland and the types of plants that grow in the various habitats, the sponsors took Julie to Finland to visit working forests and also to see an ancient area that had never been touched by man. She was both inspired and fascinated to observe the differences and especially to see the effects of man's intervention. She was also able to study the various types of undergrowth and the areas of peat bog and rocky outcrops that occurred naturally, features that she wished to reproduce within the garden.

The sponsors had originally intended to select a number of forest trees and to bring them across on one of the large container ships used to carry paper. Then they discovered that there were very strict controls on importing live trees,

above: the clearing next to the cabin is filled with a subtle abundance of cultivated and wild flowers, including ox-eye daisies, the vivid purplish-pink *Gladiolus communis* subsp. *byzantinus*, *Veronica gentianoides*, scabious, *Camassia leichtlinii* and meadow cranesbill (*Geranium pratense*).

mainly because of a nasty little beetle known as the Northern Bark Beetle, which was not a welcome visitor. So they were faced with having to find a similar pine and spruce forest in the UK! Fortunately, a large tree-moving company, Ruskins, knew of such a piece of woodland in Surrey; an area of pine and spruce plantation, it had been planted long ago for timber and now lay abandoned. Perfect. A number of trees were selected and on a clear area of land alongside the woodland, a rough layout of the garden was plotted. The trees were temporarily replanted, ensuring that the maximum amount of root was dug up with each tree. It was the middle of winter and approximately six months away from when the trees would be needed.

The next challenge was the log cabin. It seems that throughout Finland there are many such cabins or small hay barns, no longer used by the farmers and just left to fall down. So one was selected, carefully taken apart and flat-packed for shipping.

In order to re-create the small hollows of peaty bogland, a trip to Ireland was arranged. Careful research revealed an area complete with layers of the living sphagnum moss and wonderfully coloured lichens in greys, greens and reds. The area was cut up into cubes and packed into plastic boxes ready to be flown over. To portray the characteristic woodland rocky outcrops, large pieces of weathered granite were sourced from a Scottish quarry.

Now all was complete and ready to be assembled on site. First the forest trees were brought in on six huge flatbed articulated lorries, which only just managed to squeeze in between the grand brick piers of the main entrance gateway. A large crane was used to lift each tree into place. The whole process proved to be very nerve-racking, especially when trying to lift the trees, each weighing several tons, from the horizontal to the vertical. The first two were very nearly dropped when their metal rootball cages shattered. When the trees were in position the granite boulders were brought in and lifted into place.

The cabin was then unpacked and reassembled mid-way up the slope, nestling at the edge of the trees. In front of the cabin is a simple decked veranda with a traditional Scandinavian Arts and Crafts chair and a group of treated papier-mâché plant pots, all on loan from the Swedish landscape architect Ulf Nordfjel. These items reinforced the underlying message that everything in the garden was ultimately derived from the tree.

Running down from the cabin are broad timber tread and woodchip mulch steps that lead to a weathered timber boardwalk alongside the damp peaty hollow. Here there are clumps of grasses and acid-loving perennials; the dancing heads of the cotton grass *(Eriophorum angustifolium)* bob alongside the tall spikes of golden-brown flowers of the woodrush *(Luzula sylvatica)*.

Leading up into the forest is a winding grass pathway lined with a mixture of grasses and flowering perennials growing happily in the open, meadow-like clearings or in dappled shade. The course of the path is picked out by the sunny yellow of *Geum* 'Georgenburg', supported by the bright blue bugle *(Ajuga reptans* 'Catlin's Giant').

above: a classic Scandinavian Arts and Crafts chair looks out over the forest clearing.

Trees
Betula pendula (silver birch)
Picea abies (Norway spruce)
Pinus sylvestrs (Scots pine)
Salix caprea (goat willow)
Sorbus aucuparia (mountain ash)

Plants for shade/semi-shade
Ajuga reptans (bugle)
Alchemilla mollis
Campanula persicifolia (peach-leaved bellflower
Carex pendula (pendulous sedge)
Carex sylvatica (wood sedge)
Convallaria majalis (lily of the valley)
Corydalis flexuosa 'Père David'
Deschampsia cespitosa (tufted hair grass)

Digitalis purpurea (foxgloves)
Euphorbia amygdaloides (wood spurge)
Galium odoratum (sweet woodruff)
Geranium robertianum (herb Robert)
Hesperis matronalis (sweet rocket)
Silene dioica (red campion)
Teucrium scorodonia (wood sage)
Viola tricolor (heartsease)

Plants for damp/peaty areas
Eriophorum angustifolium (cotton grass)
Filipendula ulmaria
Geum rivale (water avens)
Iris sibirica 'Tropic Night'
Luzula sylvatica (greater woodrush)

Lythrum salicaria
Menyanthes trifoliata (bogbean)
Myosotis scorpioides (forget-me-not)
Persicaria bistorta
Tiarella cordifolia

Plants for open aspects
Achillea 'Moonshine'
Alopecurus pratensis (meadow foxtail)
Anthoxanthium odoratum (sweet vernal grass)
Calluna vulgaris
Camassia leichtlinii
Centranthus ruber (red valerian)
Festuca ovina (sheep's fescue)
Geranium pratense (meadow cranesbill)

Geum 'Georgenburg'
Gladiolus communis subsp. *byzantinus*
Iris 'Amber Queen'
Leucanthemum vulgare (ox-eye daisy)
Myrrhis odoratus (sweet cicely)
Nepeta 'Six Hills Giant'
Ranunculus acris (meadow buttercup)
Reseda luteola (weld)
Salvia pratensis (meadow clary)
Salvia X *superba*
Scabious spp.
Tradescantia X *andersoniana*
Trifolium pratensis (red clover)
Verbascum 'Gainsborough'
Veronica gentianoides

While she was on her travels, Julie had noticed the use of a traditional style of rustic fencing made from birch, where the timber is stripped of its bark and the pieces of bark are then used to lash the lengths of timber together. A father and son team were flown over from Finland especially to ensure that it was done in the time-honoured fashion. In order to make the bark supple, it was first necessary to 'smoke' it over a fire while it was still moist with sap after stripping. A small wood fire was duly lit and the smoking carried out – much to the consternation of the Health & Safety officials who thought there was a mini forest fire under way!

The quality and authenticity of the garden was borne out by the delighted and emotional reactions of the Scandinavian visitors, who were quite overwhelmed when they unexpectedly came upon such a beautiful re-creation of a beloved part of their countryside.

below: red campion and sweet cicely jostle for position next to the rustic fencing, with bright yellow *Geum* 'Georgenburg' in the foreground.
opposite: *Iris sibirica* grows in the water of the woodland pool. Behind it, *Persicaria bistorta*, *Tiarella cordifolia*, forget-me-nots and foxgloves.

A CELEBRATION OF GERTRUDE JEKYLL

above: the iris rill is a practical way to include the charm of a water feature in a relatively small garden.

opposite: height is an important element of any herbaceous border. In this planting it is achieved with the rich purple *Iris sibirica* 'Caesar's Brother', along with foxgloves, aquilegias and lupins.

This garden was timed to celebrate the 150th anniversary of Gertrude Jekyll's birth in 1843; but it is difficult to talk of Jekyll alone without reference to the other half of the unique partnership, namely the architect Sir Edwin Lutyens. It was he who planned the overall design and structure of the gardens to which Jekyll put on the 'flesh'; the planting that brought the whole creation to life. Her early training as an artist and a lifetime spent painting gave her a special eye for colour and form. Here we see how the designer Jane Fearnley-Whittingstall has managed to condense into a relatively small space various aspects of their respective talents.

The backbone of the garden is the iris rill, a shallow channel approximately 300mm (12 inches) deep with water continuously flowing through, making ideal growing conditions for the mixture of moisture-loving iris and trollius. The rill empties into one of Jekyll's favourite features, the circular dipping pond with its inner ring of steps. It isn't purely decorative; it is indeed meant for dipping watering cans into, and even when the water level is low you can step down and fill the can with ease.

The paving pattern is typical of Lutyens, with a mixture of natural stone and brick. The stone radiates out from the pool, with a subtle change in level taking you up to the brick pathways on either side, fronting the broad herbaceous borders. In one corner of the garden a traditional, open-sided Lutyens-style summerhouse has a green oak pergola extending away from it, a charming framework for the climbing roses. The creamy white of *Rosa* 'Rambling Rector' blends perfectly with the butter-yellow of *Rosa* 'Emily Gray', two of the fragrant varieties loved by Gertrude Jekyll.

The garden is enclosed by a high brick wall, here and there pierced by 'portholes' ringed by a circle of terracotta roof tiles. This subtle linking of the garden to the house is another of Lutyens' trademarks.

The abundance of herbaceous planting is typical of Jekyll's style, with strong hot colours carefully juxtaposed with cooler, paler tones; the reds of *Euphorbia griffithii* 'Fireglow' and the bright yellow of *Aquilegia longissima* running through to the lavenders and blues of *Iris sibirica*, *Aquilegia alpina* and the deep purple-blue of *Lupinus* 'Thundercloud'. Jekyll also knew the value of foliage: the delicate leaves of aquilegia sit pleasingly next to slender iris and the pointed ovals of the foxgloves. The overall effect is a garden that is both stimulating and relaxing.

Herbaceous borders

Alchemilla mollis
Aquilegia alpina
Aquilegia longissima
Crambe maritima (sea kale)
Cynara cardunculus (cardoon)
Digitalis purpurea (foxglove)
Euphorbia griffithii 'Fireglow'
Euphorbia characias subsp. *wulfenii*
Geranium 'Johnson's Blue'

Hemerocallis 'Hyperion'
Hesperis matronalis (sweet rocket)
Hosta sieboldiana var. *elegans*
Hydrangea arborescens 'Annabelle'
Iris sibirica 'Caesar's Brother'
Lavandula angustifolia 'Munstead'
Lavandula stoechas subsp.
    pedunculata (French lavender)
Lupinus 'Thundercloud'
Omphalodes cappadocica

Paeonia lactiflora 'Sarah
    Bernhardt'
Parthenocissus henryana
Polemonium caeruleum (Jacob's
    ladder)
Polystichum setiferum
Rosa 'Albertine' (rambler)
Rosa 'Emily Gray' (rambler)
Rosa 'Gertrude Jekyll' (shrub)
Rosa 'Rambling Rector'

Viola cornuta 'Lilacina'
Zantedeschia aethiopica
    'Crowborough'

Rill and pool

Iris laevigata
Iris sibirica
Myosotis scorpioides
Primula chungensis
Trollius X *cultorum* 'Earliest of All'

LE BOSQUET DE CHANEL

above: poised within a beech niche, the golden Venus de' Medici forms the main focal point of the garden.
opposite: the central parterre features an intricate design in clipped box.

This garden was created as a tribute to one of the unique women of the 20th century, someone who has left a lasting impression on the world of fashion, the couturier and perfumer 'Coco' Chanel (1883–1971). It is a place of charm and elegance, reflecting her style and personality, and in particular it celebrates her love of white flowers; whenever possible, she would surround herself with them, especially her favourite, the white camellia.

Karl Lagerfeld, head of fashion at Chanel, commissioned the designer Tom Stuart-Smith to create a white garden, in the Baroque style. Tom visualized this *bosquet*, or grove, as being part of a larger setting, with the main focal axis ending at this point. The inspiration is very much from the great climax of Baroque garden design in 17th-century France, which culminated in the work of Jacques Boyceau and, especially, André Le Nôtre at the châteaux of Vaux-le-Vicomte, Fontainebleau and Versailles.

Around two sides, the garden is viewed through magnificent arches of trained beech. The designer had seen these some four years before the garden was created, in a tree nursery in southern Germany, and had stored them away in his memory bank for use at a later date. Once this garden was conceived – a

year before the show – the trees were shipped to England so that they could be paired up and grown in together, each one positioned exactly on a mock-up of the garden layout within a giant glasshouse at Waterer's nursery.

Finely clipped box hedges contain mixed borders of flowering shrubs and perennials, all on the theme of white. Masses of the white bearded *Iris* 'White City' and *Aquilegia vulgaris* 'Nivea' mingle with the spiked flower heads of *Verbascum bombyciferum* 'Mont Blanc' and the silver-grey leaves of the Scotch thistle (*Onopordum acanthium*). A fragrant lilac (*Syringa vulgaris* 'Madame Lemoine'), with its large panicles of double white flowers, mixes with the lace-caps of *Viburnum sargentii* 'Onondaga' and great drifts of white foxgloves. At their feet are perennial geraniums (*G. sylvaticum* 'Album', *G. phaeum* 'Album' and *G. clarkei* 'Kashmir White') and carpets of aromatic woodruff (*Galium odoratum*). And then, of course, there are Coco Chanel's beloved camellias: *C.* 'Mathotiana Alba', *C.* 'Nobilissima', *C.* 'Serenade' et al. The problem was to have them flowering towards the middle of May, when the garden was to be on show. In order to achieve this they were kept in cold storage so as to hold them back from flowering at their natural time at the beginning of the year.

At the centre of the garden is the exquisitely designed *parterre de broderie*, with the repeating fleur de lys and interlocking ciphers of the Chanel 'C'. Just over 2,000 box plants were planted through a template into 30 numbered trays so that the whole thing could be lifted and transported to the site. It could then be reassembled like a giant jigsaw puzzle, each part fitting snugly alongside the next and requiring the minimum of trimming to give it the appearance of a long-established feature. The gravel path and infill screened out any sign of the trays. To ensure that the plants were in perfect condition they were planted out a year in advance, allowing them to be fed and trimmed as required.

You can enter the garden at two points, in each case up a small flight of beautifully detailed York stone steps. Originally the intention had been to make them out of Purbeck marble, but the quarry flooded, and although everyone was prepared to wait as long as possible, the decision to switch to York stone finally had to be made in order to get them completed on time.

Each point of entry has its own focal feature. The first is a handsome bench seat made in the style of 18th-century architect, designer and landscape gardener William Kent by the furniture maker Maureen Brown. This is placed within the niche of one of the beech arches and has an eye-catching clipped box sphere 'floating' above and behind the bench.

But undoubtedly the focal point of the whole garden is the stunning gilded figure of Venus; it is the Venus de' Medici, a famous statue from antiquity. During the 18th century there had been a similar statue within the rotunda at the celebrated landscape gardens of Stowe, Buckinghamshire, of which the poet Gilbert West (1703–56) wrote: '...Lo!, in the centre of this beauteous scene, Glitters beneath her Dome the Cyprian Queen...' The statue had disappeared in the early 19th century, and the National Trust was looking for another, to restore the rotunda to its former glory. The version we see here is a cast of the one at Blenheim Palace by the sculptor Massimiliano Soldani Benzi, which had been identified as being closest to the one that had once stood at Stowe. Chanel paid for the gilding on the understanding that the National Trust would then use it at Stowe. There were murmurings that the highly gilded figure was a little vulgar, but the designer insists that it is very much in the spirit of the Baroque period; indeed, Louis XIV, the Sun King, would have been outraged at the suggestion that his glorious statues should in any way be aged or patinated!

The story of this garden has a happy ending: it was not destroyed at the end of the week, but was transported to Ireland, where it can now be found as part of the larger gardens of Stackallan, Co. Meath.

above: the elegant garden bench is based on an early 18th-century design by William Kent.
opposite: a 'white garden' *par excellence*; the planting includes irises, aquilegias, verbascum, euphorbia, and the silvery leaves of the Scotch thistle.

THE MARINER'S GARDEN

This garden is exceptional not only because of its theme but also because it was constructed by the final-year students of Merrist Wood College in Surrey. Over many years, the college has built up quite a reputation for the quality of its gardens, having won 11 gold medals in all. For the most part, this has been due to the guiding hand of principal tutor Geoff Ace, who has a wonderful eye for detail and the ability to achieve that special feeling of a sense of place. This design was by Merrist Wood student James Dixon, who wanted to create a secluded retreat for a retired mariner who had spent his early years as a fisherman. It would be somewhere he could while away the hours on a warm summer's day, gently swinging in his hammock, remembering times past, of high seas and bountiful catches.

The old-style cane lobster pots and fine-mesh fishing nets are keepsakes from the past; today's plastic equivalents are aesthetically far less pleasing. The breakwater timbers were rescued from a replacement sea defence project somewhere on the south coast of England and their authenticity is complemented by the granite setts, which are commonplace at the seaside and ideal for the paved terrace and garden.

Probably the most extraordinary part of the garden is the seashore, complete with its flotsam and marram grass and the gently lapping sea. The water was genuinely salty, to encourage the seaweed and to give a salty tang to the air! A 'wave machine' was made using a simple electric pump that the students geared down and attached to a short plank of wood. This was enough to produce the very slight movement required. The whole thing was situated out of sight under a piece of decking and cost a fraction of the price of any commercially available version.

Planting is typical of the seaside, with plants selected for their tolerance of salt-laden winds. The horizontal lines of the prostrate junipers contrast with the rounder forms of the corokia and olearias and the spiky leaves of the variegated phalaris (often known as ribbon grass or gardener's garters) and purple cordylines.

Apart from its nostalgic appeal, this garden would be ideal for someone who lived inland but wished that they lived by the sea. On with the bikini and sunscreen lotion, out with the deckchair. And with the gentle lap of the waves on your very own seashore, you can lie back and dream…perhaps you can even hear the seagulls.

A DECORATIVE KITCHEN GARDEN

above: the pavilion supports a multitude of climbers, including the golden hop (*Humulus lupulus* 'Aureus'), the grape vine (*Vitis* 'Brant') and the rambling rose *Rosa* 'Goldfinch'.

opposite: a witty centrepiece to a kitchen garden, the fountain was cast from a real specimen of Brussels sprout.

This garden explores the possibilities of a vegetable garden that is both practical and beautiful. The designer Rupert Golby wished to create the sort of garden that feels like home; it is very much a productive, working, kitchen garden that also happens to look attractive. To achieve this, he has planted an abundance of different varieties of vegetables and soft fruits mixed in with a host of culinary herbs and flowers ideal for cutting – a traditional cottage planting taken to this glorious conclusion.

The setting is the corner of a large walled kitchen garden, but the ideas would work just as well in a more modest situation, whether rural or urban, where they could be scaled down to fit a small walled back garden to make the most fruitful use of a limited space.

On two sides, ancient walls of red brick provide all-important shelter. Nestling in the corner, a beautifully constructed open-sided pavilion is the ideal place to sit and take a well-earned break. The roof of the pavilion, which is

above: paths radiate out from the fountain, giving access to a great abundance of fresh, home-grown vegetables and soft fruits.

made up of weathered Cotswold stone tiles rescued from a derelict farmhouse, is being happily colonized by the aptly named roof houseleek (*Sempervivum tectorum*) with its purple-tipped leaves and clusters of star-shaped reddish-purple flowers. The two supporting classic style columns – new but tempered to appear old – are ideal supports for climbers: the golden hop (*Humulus lupulus* 'Aureus') scrambles up one and a vine (*Vitis* 'Brant') up the other.

A terrace of random York stone paving leads off to left and right onto rolled cinder pathways that run parallel to the garden walls. Against the walls, trained espaliers of apple and pear are interlaced with a multitude of sweet-smelling rambling roses – the double rosettes of *Rosa* 'Sander's White Rambler' and the fully double carmine pink of *Rosa* 'Madame Grégoire Staechelin' – and the bright mauve-pink of the late-flowering *Clematis* 'Comtesse de Bouchaud'. At their feet is a typical mixture of vegetables and flowering perennials. The delightfully named lettuce 'Sangria' and the blood-red leaves of the beetroot 'Bulls Blood' form a richly coloured tapestry with the purple-leaved salvia and

Iris 'Rose Violet'. The feathery bronze-leaved fennel and the velvety deep crimson-maroon of *Rosa* 'Tuscany Superb' pick up the general colour theme.

Directly in front of the terrace at the heart of the garden is a large round pool in red brick, with special half-rounds as a coping, raised to sitting height. At the centre is a bronze fountain, a wonderful homage to the humble Brussels sprout by the sculptor Simon Allison. In order to create the moulds for the casting it was necessary to use a real specimen where the 'sprouts' were still tight. This proved to be difficult due to a mild winter and a late start. One was finally tracked down in a cold corner of a local farmer's field. Each sprout and leaf was then carefully separated and a mould made of each. They were then cast in bronze and re-assembled; with hollow stems and cupped leaves, they created the perfect form for a three-stemmed cascade fountain.

A mixture of old brick and quarry tiles provides the surface for the pathways dividing the three main planting beds. The longest path takes you under a hazel archway that was constructed on site. The longer cut lengths of hazel are stuck

above: cabbages and chives line the cinder pathway. Behind them the feathery leaves of bronze fennel mingle with *Nepeta sibirica*, sweet peas and the sparkling blue of borage and cornflower.

above: bees help to pollinate flowers and vegetables and, in return for their feast of nectar, will provide the keen self-sufficient gardener with a supply of honey.
opposite: marigolds (*Calendula* 'Orange King') provide a striking contrast to these vivid ornamental cabbages, 'Christmas Mix', and are a valuable addition to the kitchen garden: the petals are edible and can be scattered over salads.

into the ground to make the hoops, with thinner strips threaded horizontally to form a frame for a favourite variety of runner bean, 'Painted Lady'. At their feet the candy-striped blooms of *Rosa gallica* 'Versicolor' alternate with the fragrant, ruffled rose-pink flowers of *Paeonia* 'Sarah Bernhardt'; this planting is repeated around the inner edge of all the beds to give a sense of visual continuity among the profusion of colour and form. To reinforce the continuity, a blue fringe of the catmint *Nepeta* 'Six Hills Giant' runs around the edge of the pathways.

The beds themselves are a positive cornucopia of soft fruits, vegetables and scented herbs – such as lemon balm, sage and thyme – interspersed with familiar cottage plants such as lavender, verbascum, digitalis, delphinium and campanula. In two of the beds are large octagonal fruit cages made in the style of mediaeval tented pavilions, with cast-iron finials and sides of dark netting. The sides are made from fine-mesh fishing nets picked up from an antique shop; today's synthetic mesh doesn't hang nearly as well. In one cage is a mixture of blackcurrant bushes, strawberries and an old-fashioned variety of blackberry, *Rubus* 'Parsley Leaved'. In the other are standards of the redcurrant 'Red Lake', more strawberries, and a stand of raspberry canes of the variety 'Glencova'.

Vegetables both ordinary and extraordinary fill the beds. Lettuce varieties include 'Little Gem' and 'Lollo Rossa'; joining them on the role call of sweet abundance are cabbages 'Greyhound' and 'Red Drumhead', carrots 'Early French Frame', the leaf beet 'Rhubarb Chard', courgettes 'Golden Zucchini', Florence fennel 'Sirio', globe and Jerusalem artichokes, the purple-flushed leek 'St Victor', shallots 'Atlantic', sweetcorn 'Earlibelle' and baby beetroot, turnips and squash. Standing sentinel over these fruits of the earth are tall hazel tepees of sweet-smelling, blue and pink sweet peas.

The essential players in this small corner of Eden are the busy humming bees, housed in traditional lap-boarded hives. Feasting upon the host of pollinating flowers, they return to create one of nature's sweetest miracles, honey.

CHEF'S ROOF GARDEN

above: fresh vegetables, herbs and flowers for the gourmet gardener...in the foreground, a pot of scented geraniums, whose leaves can be infused in milk to make a fragrant custard, stands next to a container with a mixture of pinks and sage.

This garden is a true gourmet's delight – and who better to create it than Britain's design guru and restaurant tycoon, Sir Terence Conran? 'Vegetables are a passion of mine. I have a thriving vegetable garden at home and I love eating tomatoes fresh from the vine, asparagus plunged into boiling water moments after it has been picked. That freshness – and plants that have been grown for flavour – does so much more to satisfy the palate than the bland, greenhouse-grown vegetables sold in the supermarkets.'

So here we have the humble vegetable plot elevated to the highest level in more senses than one: it is a wonderful mix of the extraordinary and the ordinary. Alongside such staples as lettuce, celery, beetroot, French beans, and even potatoes, there are aubergines, several varieties of courgettes and tomatoes, ruby chard, Florence fennel, asparagus peas, sugar snap peas, strawberries and a fine selection of culinary herbs. And because it's conceived as a chef's kitchen garden, many of the flowers are edible – from courgette flowers to rose petals.

Being a roof garden, everything is grown in containers. A chief advantage of container planting is that you're not tied to just one soil type as you would be in a conventional garden. Most of these containers are based on a standard range of pig's troughs; they are made of galvanized steel, with an added lining of treated timber to keep them cool. Detachable thermal covers coupled with a solar-powered under-soil heating system give each planter its own micro-climate throughout the seasons. Collected rainwater also helps to provide a self-sustaining irrigation system.

The party-wall is south facing and provides the perfect situation for growing espalier fruit trees, opening up the possibility of a whole range of freshly picked fruit throughout the seasons: apricots and peaches, cherries, apples, pears, quinces and medlars. Selected varieties of grape vines add to the variety of fruits waiting to be harvested when the moment is just right. And even if home-brewing is not a vital element of the chef's self-sufficiency scheme, the common hop (*Humulus lupulus*) is an ornamental plant in its own right.

Light muslin curtains on tubular steel frames afford protection from the sun and wind as required; they also allow screening from the neighbours. Above all else, this space is for entertaining. Behind the great panes of plate glass at one end of the garden, the kitchen, in stainless steel with oak trim, is the ultimate in contemporary sophistication. The kitchen is approached by a bridge that passes over a 'moat' of shallow water. At night this is lit up for added dramatic effect.

At the heart of the garden is a generously sized dining table, ideal for evening dinner parties or the family Sunday lunch. A soft sand pit runs beneath the table. Sir Terence suggests that this is 'either for children to play in or for the adults to take off their socks and shoes and wiggle their toes in while they eat…'

above: the compact cabbage 'Minicole' and the sugar snap peas are ready for picking. In the next container, globe artichokes rise from a bed of catmint.

There is a total of 46 containers, planted as follows:

1 Arum lily (*Zantedeschia aethiopica*); English cress
2 Iris
3 Cardoon
4 Chicory; arum lily (*Zantedeschia aethiopica* 'Green Goddess')
5 French beans 'Purple Tepee'
6 Dwarf French beans; purple sage (*Salvia officinalis* Purpurascens Group)
7 Creeping thyme; asparagus
8 Kohlrabi 'Purple Vienna'; *Geranium macrorrhizum*
9 Lettuce varieties
10 Red chard; sorrel 'Buckler Leaf'
11 Asparagus peas
12 Strawberries ('Eros', 'Symphony', 'Hapil', 'Elsanta')
13 Beetroot ('Avon Early', 'Boltardy')
14 Purple kale 'Redbor'
15 Potatoes 'Charlotte'
16 Aubergines

17 Garden peas 'Cavalier'; sweet cicely
18 Bronze fennel (*Foeniculum vulgare* 'Purpureum'); poppies (*Papaver rhoeas*)
19 Lettuce varieties
20 Tomatoes 'Tumbler'
21 Lettuce 'Red Salad Bowl'
22 Spinach; scented pelargonium 'Lady Plymouth'; black peppermint
23 Tomatoes 'Tigerella'
24 Chard 'Rainbow'
25 Radishes 'French Breakfast'
26 Yellow courgettes
27 Broad beans; *Bellis perennis* 'Miss Mason'
28 Salsify; *Viola odorata*
29 Kale 'Nero di Toscana'; chives
30 Florence fennel 'Zeno Fino'; variegated applemint
31 Celery 'Golden Blanching'; marjoram
32 French beans 'Robsplash Climbing'
33 Lettuce varieties
34 Yellow cherry tomatoes
35 Kohlrabi 'Green Vienna'; catmint (*Nepeta* x *faassenii*)

36 Sugar snap peas
37 Artichokes 'Green Globe'; catmint
38 Sage (*Salvia officinalis* 'Icterina'); *Dianthus* 'Pike's Pink'
39 Courgettes 'Italian Round'; *Achillea* 'Coronation Gold'; winter savory (*Satureia montana*)
40 Angelica; golden marjoram
41 Green courgettes
42 Lemon balm; French tarragon
43 French beans 'Rob Roy Climbing'
44 Lettuce varieties
45 Sage; sorrel 'Buckler Leaf'; *Rosa* 'Schneezwerg'; *Artemisia* 'Silver Queen'
46 Cabbage 'Minicole'

In front of the kitchen are two bay trees (*Laurus nobilis*). Along one side of the garden are planted espalier fruit trees: apple, pear, apricot, medlar, peach, quince, cherry. Climbers include varieties of vine and the common hop (*Humulus lupulus*).

ROCKS AND WATERFALLS

above: the water emerges from a 'forest' of mixed conifers, their upright habits forming a subtle counterbalance to the horizontal line of the series of cascades. Waterside planting is minimal: a clump of *Dicentra* 'Snowflakes' flourishes in the shade of a steep drop in the rocks; *Trollius chinensis* 'Golden Queen' brightens the foreground.

Rock gardens with waterfalls are among the most difficult to create in such a way as to make them appear perfectly natural, as if they have been there for ever. In nature, such features may have taken hundreds, thousands or indeed millions of years to evolve. And without doubt the art of making a really effective rock and water garden comes from observing just how nature does it, with many types of rock and in many different settings. It is important to observe how the rock lies, for each piece of rock, no matter what its size, has a natural 'grain' according to how it was formed; whether by enormous pressure over many aeons or by the solidification of a molten eruption from the earth's core.

Water will always take the shortest route, and it takes skill and a good eye to create extra interest. In a garden, the water could drop from a series of different heights, or be sent in different directions as it cascades down the length of the fall.

Here we have three splendid examples by a very experienced designer and practitioner in the art, Doug Knight, often referred to as the 'King of Rock' (apologies to Elvis fans). He gets much of his inspiration when he is travelling around such areas as the Yorkshire Dales and Moors, the Lake District and the rugged coastline of North Wales, where the rocky outcrops of the great mountains extend down to the sea.

The first garden uses slate from a quarry in North Wales. The stone had been quarried more than 300 years ago and had lain in a deserted part of the quarry gathering a natural bloom of moss. Extra care had to be taken so as not to disturb this during transportation to the site. The shapes and 'lie' of the rocks has been exploited to create a simple series of wide drops with varying falls.

Slate has also been used in the second garden, but this example, from the same, vast quarry in North Wales, has a greater amount of spar in it, giving it a

below: prostrate junipers echo the shape of the rocks as they tumble down the slope, while the leaves of *Iris japonica* 'Variegata' and variegated hostas join *Ranunculus montanus* 'Molten Gold' and *Carex elata* 'Aurea' to create a fresh yellow and green theme.

distinctive marbled effect. This can present a problem if plants are positioned too close to these areas, as the sun is reflected up on to the underside of the leaves and can burn them. The huge slabs of rock have been positioned so that their 'grain' always lies at the same, slight angle as it works its way down the slope; the water is 'squeezed' between the gaps, forming deep pools along the way. The 'source' of the waterfall appears beautifully natural: in the distance you glimpse a long line of water running in from the dark shadows of the mixed planting of rhododendrons and conifers.

Great slabs of Coniston rock from the Lake District have been used in the third example. Here they are heavily layered across a large area, with a number of streams running down the slope. Slate shale has been used to fill both the bottom of the pools and in between the crevices, creating a perfect growing medium for the many different varieties of alpines and succulents that tumble down the slope in a stream of pinks, yellows and greens.

below: this powerful rock garden provides a dramatic home for a great variety of alpine plants.

The final garden is by the designer David Stevens, and is called 'Rockscape'. It cleverly shows how you can turn an entire garden into a rock and water feature. Huge slabs of rock progress up the slope, providing a giant flight of steps and a simple bridge, which leads across to the paved terrace in front of the small garden building.

A garden like this cannot be built solely from a plan; you have to select your stone with care and then build up the garden by eye, creating the waterways as you go. The 'eye' in this case was a very experienced and skilled one belonging to Jack Sexton. He started with a 'key' stone weighing just over three tons, placing it at the heart of the garden and then building and extending outwards on all sides.

The water here is in a series of gently cascading rills rather than crashing falls, providing the soothing background sound of falling water. The rocks have been especially chosen and positioned to simulate the effect of water-worn courses, and are of foliated quartzite, which sparkles in the sunlight. The slabs of rock are a perfect foil for the simple but subtle areas of planting, the restrained green colour palette highlighted by touches of purple and white. In the moisture-loving groups of iris and hostas, the vertical form of the iris contrasts with the bold foliage clumps of *Hosta sieboldiana*; their leaves, in turn, are echoed in the smaller form of the adjacent drifts of *Epimedium* X *rubrum*.

above: the garden is made up of great slabs of rock laid on a rising slope, interlaced with subtle planting.

THE SPOUT GARDEN

above: shaded by the Japanese maple *Acer japonicum* 'Vitifolium', the spout is surrounded by ferns, with flashes of colour from the violet and red pokers of *Primula vialii* and the delicate cups of *Polemonium reptans* 'Blue Pearl'. *Iris pseudacorus* 'Variegata' grows in the trough itself.

opposite: the yellow-green leaves of the Indian bean tree (*Catalpa bignonioides* 'Aurea') form a focal point in any garden. Its bright colours are echoed in the euphorbia and *Alchemilla mollis* that line the path to the summer-house, over which rambles *Rosa* 'Rambling Rector'.

Inspiration for this garden takes the designer back to the days of his childhood on his father's farm, high in the Derbyshire Hills. Each morning the cows would be brought in for milking. They would walk up the lane to the old timber milking shed and stop to drink at a water trough fed by a natural spring through an old piece of galvanized pipe, referred to as the 'spout'. It was this simple picture that imprinted on the young mind and was to resurface years later. Shortly after deciding to create a garden around this memory, Roger Platts had taken over a run-down nursery. While rummaging in an area of overgrown brambles and nettles he came upon a pair of weathered oak gate posts and an old riveted galvanized water trough, perfect for his Spout Garden…it was as though some hidden hand was at work, bringing all the elements together.

The garden is laid out on a long and narrow site and set on two principle levels, with retaining walls of recycled red brick. You 'enter' from the grassy meadow at the bottom right hand corner, through an old, broken-down farm gate, and pass along an 'overgrown' track beside a gently rusting park railing entwined with a mixture of wild and cultivated flowers and the sweet scented rambling rose *Rosa* 'Albertine'.

Turning to the left you enter the lower terrace and there before you is the

right: the distant memory of a farm's old water trough and cattle shed have been spun into an enchanting garden.

above: the lower terrace is a symphony of purples and pinks, but the effect is far from over-whelming, toned down by many touches of silver-grey, white and creamy yellow. At ground level, these include the upright tufts and striped, swordlike leaves of *Sisyrinchium striatum* 'Aunt May' and, towering above the scene in the top right, the graceful tiered foliage of *Cornus alternifolia* 'Argentea'.

water spout, issuing forth into the old galvanized trough, surrounded by a pleasing mix of fresh greens and yellows – the Japanese maple *Acer japonicum* 'Vitifolium', the variegated swordlike leaves of *Iris pseudacorus* 'Variegata', the white-variegated deadnettle *Lamium maculatum* 'White Nancy', the clusters of pale yellow tubular flowers of *Phygelius aequalis* 'Yellow Trumpet' – with flashes of rich colour from *Primula vialii, Polemonium reptans* 'Blue Pearl' and *Iris sibirica*.

To one side, a simple timber bench looks across the brick paving and down the gravel track, with a wonderful abundance of flowering through the spectrum of pinks, purples and blues. A mixture of scented lavenders includes the deep purple 'Hidcote' and the French varieties *Lavandula stoechas* 'Helmsdale' and the darker 'Marshwood'. The purple theme is picked up by the spikes of *Salvia verticillata* 'Purple Rain' and the violet-blue *Salvia* x *sylvestris* 'May Night'. The silver-grey foliage of *Ozothamnus rosmarinifolius* 'Silver Jubilee' forms the perfect background for the delicate, cerise flowers of *Geranium palmatum*. Highlights come from the creamy-white heads of *Sisyrinchium striatum* 'Aunt May' and white-petalled *Cistus* x *obtusifolius*, with its pale lemon eye. Little clumps of *Artemisia schmidtiana, Thymus* 'Silver Posie' and *Thymus* 'Pink Chintz' thread their way between the bricks and gravel.

Brick steps take us up past the striking *Cornus alternifolia* 'Argentea', chosen for its tiered branches of oval, bright green, creamy white-margined leaves that turn a startling red in the autumn.

The upper terrace extends in front of the summerhouse, converted from the redundant 'cattle shelter'. It is made up of mature oak timbers all cut, jointed and pegged in the traditional way, with not a single nail or screw used. The fragrant, pale pink *Rosa* 'New Dawn' entwines its way around the oak pillars, together with the creamy white *Rosa* 'Rambling Rector', which scrambles up and over the pitched roof of old recycled 'pegged' clay tiles.

Running off to one side is a series of chunky timber pergolas, made of 'green' oak: freshly cut, unseasoned oak. Although the grain naturally opens up and 'shakes' or splits, it was traditionally used because it was, and still is, much cheaper than seasoned wood. Nonetheless, judging by the number of buildings and garden features that survive in this material, it seems to stand the test of time.

Their framework provides the perfect structure for a luxuriant mix of many more climbers: the white and pink flushed green leaves of *Actinidia kolomikta*, the creamy white scented blooms of the climbing rose *Rosa filipes* 'Kiftsgate', the blush-pink to white of *Rosa* 'Félicité Perpétue' and the pale pink of *Rosa* 'New Dawn'. The Indian bean tree (*Catalpa bignonioides* 'Aurea') provides a touch of drama with its large, fresh green, heart-shaped leaves; as a bonus, it offers large panicles of white flowers in the summer, followed by hanging clusters of exotic-looking bean pods in the autumn.

Throughout this part of the garden there is a feeling of abundant planting, still within the purple-blue-pink theme. The dramatic vertical columns of the delphiniums, especially the deep purple *Delphinium* 'Black Knight', are set against the clusters of lilac-purple flowers of *Solanum crispum* and the blues of the catmints *Nepeta* 'Six Hills Giant' and *Nepeta racemosa* 'Walker's Low'. The sweetly scented, soft pink, rounded blooms of the old Bourbon rose *Rosa* 'Reine Victoria' drift through the area, with light touches of the white valerian *Centranthus ruber* 'Albus'.

The planting is set against a backdrop of flowering shrubs such as *Viburnum opulus* 'Roseum', with its pom-pom white flowers, and *Viburnum plicatum* 'Mariesii', its tiered layers branches bedecked with white blooms. Blending into the backdrop are the vertical creamy white blooms of foxgloves, *Digitalis purpurea* f. *albiflora*.

A selection of specimen trees forms a year-round framework and includes one of the most striking of the flowering cherries, *Prunus cerasifera* 'Nigra' with its deep purple leaves and profusion of rosy-pink flowers. These colours are complemented by the bronze-crimson of the *Acer palmatum* f. *atropurpureum* and the white-variegated green leaves, tinged with pink, of the box elder, *Acer negundo* 'Flamingo', with an extra splash of colour from the brilliant red-tipped leaves of *Photinia* x *fraseri* 'Red Robin'.

This garden demonstrates in every way the art and skill of putting together a range of very different plants to create an overall feeling of harmony and beauty.

above: an old-fashioned white sink is planted with *Iris sibirica*, *Typha maxima* and *Isolepis cernua* and embraced by the lobed leaves of *Lindera obtusiloba*.

opposite: *Actinidia kolomikta*, with its pink- and white-flecked leaves, clambers up the 'green' oak pergola. The majestic delphiniums steal the scene, but are ably supported by a mixture of geraniums, the violet-blue flower spikes of *Salvia* x *superba* and the fresh greens of *Alchemilla mollis* and *Euphorbia characias* subsp. *wulfenii*.

Actinidia kolomikta	*Geranium clarkei* 'Kashmir Purple'	*Leptospermum scoparium* 'Snow Flurry'	*Rosa* 'Reine Victoria'
Ajuga reptans 'Burgundy Glow'	*Geranium* x *oxonianum* 'Claridge Druce'	*Lithodora diffusa* 'Heavenly Blue'	*Salvia* x *superba*
Alchemilla mollis	*Geranium palmatum*	*Nepeta* 'Six Hills Giant'	*Salvia* x *sylvestris* 'Mainacht'
Artemisia 'Powis Castle'	*Geranium pratense* 'Mrs Kendall Clarke'	*Nepeta* 'Walker's Low'	*Salvia verticillata* 'Purple Rain'
Artemisia schmidtiana	*Geranium sanguineum*	*Pittosporum* 'Garnettii'	*Scabiosa* 'Pink Mist'
Astrantia major rubra	*Hedera colchica* 'Sulphur Heart'	*Polemonium reptans* 'Blue Pearl'	*Sisyrinchium striatum* 'Aunt May'
Astrantia maxima	*Lamium maculatum* 'White Nancy'	*Primula vialii*	*Solanum crispum* 'Glasnevin'
Cistus x *obtusifolius*	*Lavandula angustifolia* 'Hidcote'	*Rosa* 'Félicité Perpétue' (climber)	*Thymus pseudolanuginosus*
Crambe cordifolia	*Lavandula stoechas* 'Helmsdale'	*Rosa filipes* 'Kiftsgate' (rambler)	*Thymus* 'Pink Chintz'
Digitalis purpurea f. *albiflora*	*Lavandula stoechas* 'Marshwood'	*Rosa* 'New Dawn' (climber)	*Thymus* 'Silver Posie'
Euphorbia amygdaloides var. *robbiae*		*Rosa* 'Rambling Rector'	*Viburnum plicatum* 'Mariesii'
Euphorbia characias subsp. *wulfenii*			*Viburnum opulus* 'Roseum'

THE PORTMEIRION GARDEN

above: the fountain issues from its shady niche and flows through a clump of *Ligularia dentata* before tumbling downhill.

opposite: moisture-loving plants such as the giant cowslip and the hart's-tongue fern flourish in the dappled sunlight beside the stream.

A taste of Italy, all the way from the coast of north Wales…this garden, designed by Bunny Guinness, was inspired by the beautiful and unique Italianate village and gardens of Portmeirion, created by one of Britain's most flamboyant 20th-century architects, the late Sir Clough Williams-Ellis. For those who can remember, Portmeirion was the setting for the cult TV series *The Prisoner*, filmed there in 1966–67. The village is still one of Wales' top tourist attractions.

To set the scene, the dramatic backdrop of the 12m (40ft) Observatory Tower has been faithfully reproduced from Sir Clough's original drawings. Off to one side is a façade in the sunbleached colours typical of an Italian seaside village.

Extending in front of the building is the top terrace, adorned with large glazed and terracotta pots filled with exotic flowering plants such as the crown imperial (*Fritillaria imperialis)*, its tall stem crowned by a ring of orange bell-shaped flowers. A pair of *Echium pininana*, with long, arching leaves, give promise of the great single spike of flower that will appear in the following year.

Set at the centre of the building, and forming a focal point to the garden, a recessed niche painted in rich blue contains a multi-spray fountain that provides the source for the central water cascade. Constructed from Welsh slate, it tumbles its way down through a delightful sunlit meadow of buttercups and moon daisies (*Leucanthemum vulgare*). Along the water's edge is a selection of moisture-loving plants: the delicate, pale yellow primula with its grand-sounding name – giant cowslip (*Primula florindae*) – and the shiny-leaved hart's-tongue fern (*Asplenium scolopendrium*) matching the equally shiny leaves of the *Saxifraga hirsuta* brought in especially from the Portmeirion estate. The stream finally passes between great clumps of the white arum lily (*Zantedeschia aethiopica* 'Crowborough'), with a splash of David Austin's special millennium rose 'Portmeirion', fragrant and pink and edging the tangled mass of the white rambling rose 'Seagull'; beneath these is a spiky row of *Camassia cusickii* with their delicate pale blue blooms.

The stream disappears from sight beneath the paving of the lower pool surround. This is made up of a bold mix of cut stone and slate with infill panels of traditional pebbling. Featured around the pool are a number of large terracotta pots filled to abundance with the blue-flowered African lily (*Agapanthus africanus*). The embossed and decorated pots were specially commissioned from the renowned Whichford Pottery on the edge of the Cotswolds.

On either side of the pool are framed archways made up in wrought iron and topped with castings of the legendary phoenix, decorated in the typically Portmeirion finishes of verdigris and gold. One of the arches frames a lead cherub on loan from the estate; the other leads through to winding stone steps that take you back up to the top terrace through a mixed woodland area featuring some of the temperate and hardy exotic plants to be found at Portmeirion, a mixture that reflects the fact that the Gulf Stream passes close by.

The basic framework of trees that help to protect the estate are species typical of the temperate zone: the oaks (*Quercus robur*), the silver birch (*Betula pendula*) and the wild cherry (*Prunus avium*). Set among these are a number of

below: *Rosa* 'Seagull' climbs over the yew hedge, while a cherub peeps out from beneath the spectacular evergreen leaves of *Rhododendron sinogrande*.

left and below: attention to detail is always a key to success at the Chelsea Flower Show. The tower was based on the original drawings by Clough Williams-Ellis, who began building Portmeirion village in Wales in 1925.

more exotic varieties: the Australian tree ferns *(Dicksonia antarctica)* contrasting with the bold, architectural, sword-like forms of the silver-grey *Astelia nervosa*, the purple *Phormium tenax* Purpureum Group and the yellow-green *Phormium tenax* 'Variegatum'. Swaying stems of the black bamboo *(Phyllostachys nigra)* are set against the bold mass of the magnificent *Rhododendron sinogrande*, with its huge, shiny, evergreen leaves and great trusses of creamy white blooms in spring.

Around the woodland edges, loosely clipped box hedges contain smaller varieties: the exotic sparkle of the deep magenta stars of *Geranium maderense* and the simple elegance of the arching perennial sedge *(Carex pendula)*. Behind these we glimpse the upright form of *Hydrangea aspera* with its late-flowering heads of purple-blue fringed with white.

Started in 1925, Portmeirion has matured into one of Britain's most beautiful and unusual gardens, known to garden lovers the world over. Here we can experience some of its enchantment, created in just two weeks!

A JAPANESE ARTIST'S GARDEN

above: this garden sculpture was imported from Japan at the beginning of the 20th century; it has been in a private British garden ever since. Behind it stand a loquat (*Eriobotrya japonica*) and a Japanese maple (*Acer palmatum* 'Chitoseyama'); beneath them are bamboo (*Phyllostachys nigra* var. *henonis*), an evergreen azalea (*Rhododendron* 'Hinode-giri') and the bright green shock of *Hakonechloa macra* 'Aureola'.

Authentic Japanese gardens are an art form with multiple layers of meaning; it is an art that can take years to master. Recognizing this, John Van Hage chose to interpret the Japanese style in a free manner, with the idea of creating a place of tranquillity where an artist could find peace and inspiration.

A Japanese garden is often said to represent the landscape in miniature: the placement of rocks and stones may suggest mountains, lakes and rivers; the planting of mature trees – carefully pruned to keep their size and shape in perfect proportion – symbolizes the forest. Nothing is left to chance: every detail is carefully considered, yet the result must give the overall impression of being true to nature. Besides the artistic impression, elements within the garden are intended as an aid to meditation and contemplation.

Features are often deliberately designed to slow you down as you pass through the garden. Here, for example, the irises lead the eye to the front of the garden, yet it is irresistibly drawn back to the imposing horizontal lines of the artist's studio. Intermingling with the sword-like leaves of the irises, grasses such as *Festuca glauca* point the way through to the Welsh slate stepping stones.

Stepping stones are seldom placed in a straight line; again, it is the garden designer's intention to make the visitor slow down and contemplate the details.

Another typical feature of Japanese gardens is that any buildings, be they temples, tea houses or ornamental pavilions, should be integrated with the garden. One way of achieving this is by having doors that slide back to frame specific views, prescribed by the gardener. The Japanese ink paintings on either side of the doors, commissioned from Ohgen Hamanaka, provide an authentic note. Yet John also felt free to interpret his theme more loosely: he commissioned an English sculptor, Kate English, to create moon sculptures.

The artist's studio was designed by John and built off site. When it was delivered, to be craned into postion, it was not only a spectacular sight but also cause for some tension, because it was a question of millimetres as to whether it would fit through the gates of the Royal Hospital grounds. However, by the time the judges saw it, the structure, surrounded by a dense and naturalistic planting that included several Japanese maples, rhododendrons and stands of black bamboo, had acquired a very real sense of age and permanence.

above: the spectacular 80-year-old black pine (*Pinus parviflora*) has the majestic appearance of a tree many times its actual size, which has been kept in check by a very precise pruning technique. Irises are a frequent motif of Japanese gardens.

A GARDEN IN PROVENCE

above: at the heart of the border, a gnarled pomegranate tree is surrounded by a vivid planting of irises ('Blue Shimmer' and 'Deep Black'), peonies ('Arabian Prince' and 'Bunker Hill') and alliums.

There are those who consider that the 'theme' gardens are more about theatre than about gardening. This opinion seems profoundly to miss the point that gardens can, and indeed should, have a rich sense of theatre, which gives them the power to stimulate the mind and stir the emotions. Gardens need not simply be about pathways, borders and lawns. With a little imagination they can become magical places where fantasies can be indulged, dreams fulfilled. But as designer Fiona Lawrenson says, 'It has to be believable and it has to be done with conviction, if it is to work…' And here, at the scale of many of today's sub-urban gardens, she demonstrates how it is possible to create a complete 'set piece' for someone who adores Provence and who wishes to recreate a part of it to experience and enjoy as their very own.

Fiona's eye for detail has ensured that the overall impression of this garden is 100 per cent successful. This was confirmed when the Queen and Prince Philip visited the garden and declared their surprise when, on closer inspection, they realized the building was not a genuine structure but, as Fiona declared, had been entirely made up of sand and cement, MDF and chicken wire!

But to get it to look so convincing required a lot of research. Fiona and her team had made a special trip to the Provence region in order to study the style and detailing of the traditional buildings so typical of that part of France. While there, they made a point of talking with local builders and craftsmen, and the results can be seen in the way they have carried out the general stonework and in such particulars as the underside of the eaves, with its line of inverted half-round terracotta ridge tiles. They were also able to discover the ingredients that went into the distinctive paint finish that is so characteristic of that part of the Mediterranean. Pigments were purchased and the artist John Simpson, who was responsible for all the special effects, experimented until he and Fiona were satisfied that the finish was just right.

The general design is based around a cobbled courtyard that was once the centre of a bustling farm. Now the animals have gone, and peace and serenity have come in the form of the garden. On one side of the courtyard are the old farm buildings, linked to a high protective wall. An opening within this wall gives a view of the lavender fields stretching away to the horizon – a beautiful illusion created by the ancient art of trompe l'oeil.

Beneath the steps leading up to the old loft is a traditional stone water fountain, brought back from France. The water is allowed to overflow from its stone

below: shaded by a lemon tree, the table looks out over the lavender fields of Provence. The illusion of being in an old garden is enhanced by the way the over-spill from the fountain trickles across its 'well-worn' path over the cobbles.

bowl and to thread its way across the cobbles into the border. For this to work, a line of cobbles had to be laid just a shade lower than the rest, so that the water followed the required path and didn't spread all over the courtyard. A small catchment well concealed in the bed collects the water and a pump recirculates it back to the fountain.

A further note of authenticity comes from the wonderful stone-topped table and the metal chairs with their heart-shaped seats. Again, these were designed and made in Provence.

Of course, it is the planting that really brings the setting to life. To give it that Mediterranean feel there are pomegranate trees, lemon trees and gnarled olive trees, which – contrary to common belief – are surprisingly hardy. Throughout the border there is a subtle interplay of silver-grey and green foliage, in different shapes, sizes and textures. Flower colour ranges from the softer tones of the rosemarys and lavenders on into the deeper purples of the alliums and irises, reaching a crescendo in the juxtaposition of *Allium hollandicum* 'Purple Sensation' and the rich purple of *Iris* 'Deep Black'. Extra drama is introduced with the bold groups of peonies, such as *Paeonia* 'Bunker Hill' and *P.* 'Arabian Prince' with its profusion of fragrant, semi-double, rich crimson-blooms. The whole is lifted by the bright orange dots of *Geum* 'Borisii' and the coppery orange of *Verbascum* 'Helen Johnson'.

Filling the air, the scent of rosemary, lavender and the sweet-smelling perennial geraniums evoke memories of that hill-top retreat high above the Côte d'Azur.

above: beyond the olive tree we glimpse the Provençal farmhouse, its steps lined with pots of geraniums, nasturtiums, marigolds and chives.
left and far left: an old stone vessel is surrounded by lollipop balls of box, together with santolina, *Helichrysum italicum*, bronze fennel, *Onopordum acanthium* and the tall flower spires of *Veronica gentianoides* 'Tissington White' and *Verbascum* 'Helen Johnson'.

THE GREENING OF INDUSTRY

The slate workers have gone, the tramway trucks have stopped running, the water pumps and grinding wheels have seized up. The pump house is crumbling and the ironwork is starting to corrode. Nature is moving in and starting to reclaim her territory. It was the fascination of how nature recolonized these old derelict industrial sites that first set the designer, Paul Cooper, thinking about how he could translate this wondrous transformation process into the context of a wild garden. He had just moved to Wales and there he came upon a magical place where a waterfall cascaded down the face of a slate outcrop that was colonized by a remarkable selection of plants. The waterfall had been visited by the Victorians and known by the extraordinary name of '*water break its neck.*' The idea of combining the natural beauty of the waterfall and the dereliction of an abandoned slate quarry formed the inspiration for this garden. He envisaged a dramatic image in the wonderfully eccentric tradition of the folly.

The garden was to be constructed by the students of Pershore College of Horticulture and initially they were not over-enthusiastic about the prospect of creating a folly, let alone a garden, from a pile of old slate and bits of rusting iron. It was not until they saw a model of the garden and then started to source and accumulate redundant steel girders, quarry artefacts and huge slabs of slate, that they were able to visualize the scale of the project. They then began to respond very positively and feel more involved in its creation.

Along with the structure, the students were also required to research and source the different plants required. These consisted of the wild plants that would naturally occur in such an environment – such as ferns, ivy, moisture-loving plants and heathers – together with certain plants that might have started in a domestic garden and migrated into the wild, like the rhododendrons and lupins. The students had to visit sites around old quarries to find out which plants would grow where: plants that grew in and around the waterfalls...those that would grow on vertical faces in the crevices...those that would colonize the slaty shale. Every situation was observed and recorded.

The scale of the finished garden is certainly very dramatic, and the painstaking construction of the derelict pump house, with the falling water and the beautifully subtle planting lacing its way into and over every crevice and hollow, gives the feeling that it has lain abandoned for decades. So convincing was the illusion that a visitor asked if it been allowed to stay there since the previous year!

THE LATIN GARDEN

above: a variety of irises
represent the colour and
sophistication of Virgil's life in
Rome. Silver-grey foliaged plants –
such as *Phlomis fruticosa*,
Verbascum 'Arctic Summer',
Ballota pseudodictamnus and the
striking cardoon in the foreground
suggest the drier gardens of the
Mediterranean.

For years a number of designers at Chelsea have been tentatively pushing at the
door of modernism. Certain critics often comment that the designs draw too
heavily on the past, with little or no reflection of the present, even though this is
perfectly understandable given our very rich gardening heritage and the undeni-
able demand for tradition.

Well, here the door has been flung wide open and the designer Christopher
Bradley-Hole has created this unique garden, which is uncompromisingly
'modern'; both in its form and its use of materials it is very much of our time.
What is especially interesting, however, is the fact that the inspiration for the
garden is that of the life and times of the celebrated Roman poet, Publius
Vergilius Maro (70-19BC), better known as Virgil, author of the *Aeneid*. It was
the three distinct phases of his rather short, but eventful, life that provide the

underlying motif and pattern of the garden, demonstrating beautifully how a classical theme can inspire a very modern interpretation.

Faced with a blank, long, rectangular site, the design was conceived around the image of a 'box' from which most of the top and two of the sides have been cut away, the remaining side and rear formed of stout, solid walls. Within the 'box' the space is divided into three harmonious areas, alluding allegorically to the three phases of Virgil's life.

In the foreground, the first part represents his humble beginnings in the countryside. Here we have a scree of limestone chippings with randomly planted Mediterranean herbs, typical of the open ground areas around the old farm buildings of northern Italy. Fragrant marjoram, rosemary and thyme intermingle with purple fennel and salvias. Four tall, clipped bay trees and a mature pomegranate, especially brought in from Tuscany, contribute a feeling of timelessness and stability.

Straight as a Roman road, a path of cedar wood decking runs the length of the garden, leading us through an imposing, square, off-white plastered archway, into the second phase of Virgil's life, that came with the success of the *Eclogues*; a life of sophistication and affluence in the city of Rome. The streamlined elegance of the glass and steel pavilion contrasts with the much more vibrantly coloured planting in this area. Representing the tree-lined streets of the city, a formal line of hornbeams leads one across a glass bridge spanning a sheet of water symbolizing the River Tiber. To one side is the mountain source, a stepped cascade, made up of contrasting bluish Hornton and white Portland stone. The water extends the full width of the garden; as it becomes calmer it reflects the play of light into the pavilion's interior. Here the stylish cast-aluminium furniture stands on a floor of polished Portland stone; there is a hint of fresh citrus aroma from a large standard lemon tree set in a custom-designed container made from birch-faced marine ply.

The planting throughout this garden is very much in the 'new perennial' style that has been developing in a number of European countries. It consists mostly of herbaceous plants, used in a naturalistic and ecological way, so that

Area A

Allium azureum
Angelica archangelica
Artemisia pontica
Calendula officinalis
Cichorium intybus f. album
Convolvulus cneorum
Foeniculum vulgare
Foeniculum vulgare 'Purpureum'
Laurus nobilis (standards)
Melianthus major
Origanum vulgare
Rosmarinus officinalis
Salvia lavandulifolia
Salvia officinalis
Salvia officinalis Purpurascens Group
Thymus serpyllum var. albus
Thymus serpyllum coccineus

Area B

Acaena microphylla 'Kupferteppich'
Achillea 'Moonshine'
Allium aflatunense
Allium christophii
Allium 'Gladiator'
Allium 'Lucy Ball'
Allium hollandicum 'Purple Sensation'
Allium 'Rien Poortvliet'
Allium schoenoprasum white
Amsonia ciliata
Amsonia tabernaemontana var. salicifolia
Ballota pseudodictamnus
Camassia leichtlinii 'Semiplena'

Carpinus betulus 'Fastigiata' (tall standards)
Catananche caerulea
Cephalaria gigantea
Cynara cardunculus
Euphorbia dulcis 'Chameleon'
Euphorbia cyparissias 'Fens Ruby'
Euphorbia × martinii
Euphorbia seguieriana subsp. niciciana
Ferula communis subsp. glauca
Geranium phaeum 'Lily Lovell'
Geranium pratense
Geranium sanguineum var. striatum
Geranium 'Spinners'
Iris 'Action Front'
Iris 'Black Swan'
Iris 'Jane Phillips'
Iris 'Kent Pride'
Iris pallida subsp. pallida
Iris 'Rajah'
Iris 'White Owl'
Knautia macedonica
Lotus hirsutus
Lupinus chamissonis
Nectaroscordum siculum
Onoclea sensibilis
Phlomis fruticosa
Phlomis russeliana
Rosa 'William Lobb'
Salvia argentea
Sesleria nitida
Stachys macrantha 'Superba'
Verbascum 'Arctic Summer'

Area C

Acaena microphylla 'Kupferteppich'
Aquilegia alpina
Aquilegia 'Port Wine'
Aquilegia vulgaris 'Ruby Port'
Aquilegia vulgaris 'William Guinness'
Astrantia major 'Claret'
Carpinus betulus 'Fastigiata'
Corylus avellana
Dianthus barbatus 'Nigrescens'
Geranium × cantabrigiense 'Cambridge'
Geranium nodosum
Geranium renardii
Iris 'Indian Chief'
Iris 'Right Royal'
Iris 'Solid Mahogany'
Iris 'Superstition'
Iris 'Tall Chief'
Knautia macedonica
Leucanthemum vulgare
Lonicera × italica
Lotus corniculatus
Rubus 'Emerald Spreader'
Sambucus nigra 'Thundercloud'
Thalictrum minus adiantifolium
Thalictrum aquilegiifolium var. album
Thalictrum flavum subsp. glaucum
Thalictrum rochebruneanum
Trifolium rubens

Area D

Anthriscus sylvestris 'Ravenswing'
Astrantia major rubra

Astrantia major 'Shaggy'
Campanula rotundifolia
Cardamine pratensis
Chaerophyllum hirsutum 'Roseum'
Chelidonium majus
Cirsium rivulare 'Atropurpureum'
Corylus avellana
Cupressus sempervirens 'Stricta'
Dryopteris filix-mas
Filipendula vulgaris 'Grandiflora'
Geranium macrorrhizum 'Album'
Geranium phaeum 'Album'
Lychnis flos-cuculi
Pilosella aurantiaca
Plantago major 'Rubrifolia'
Polemonium caeruleum
Polemonium 'Sapphire'
Polypodium vulgare
Rosa 'Sander's White Rambler'
Sanguisorba minor
Syringa meyeri var. spontanea 'Palibin'
Thalictrum rochebruneanum
Viburnum opulus 'Compactum'

Area E

Acanthus spinosus
Artemisia abrotanum
Festuca amethystina
Iris pallida subsp. pallida
Phillyrea angustifolia
Punica granatum
Rosa glauca
Rosmarinus officinalis
Sesleria caerulea
Vitis vinifera (standards)

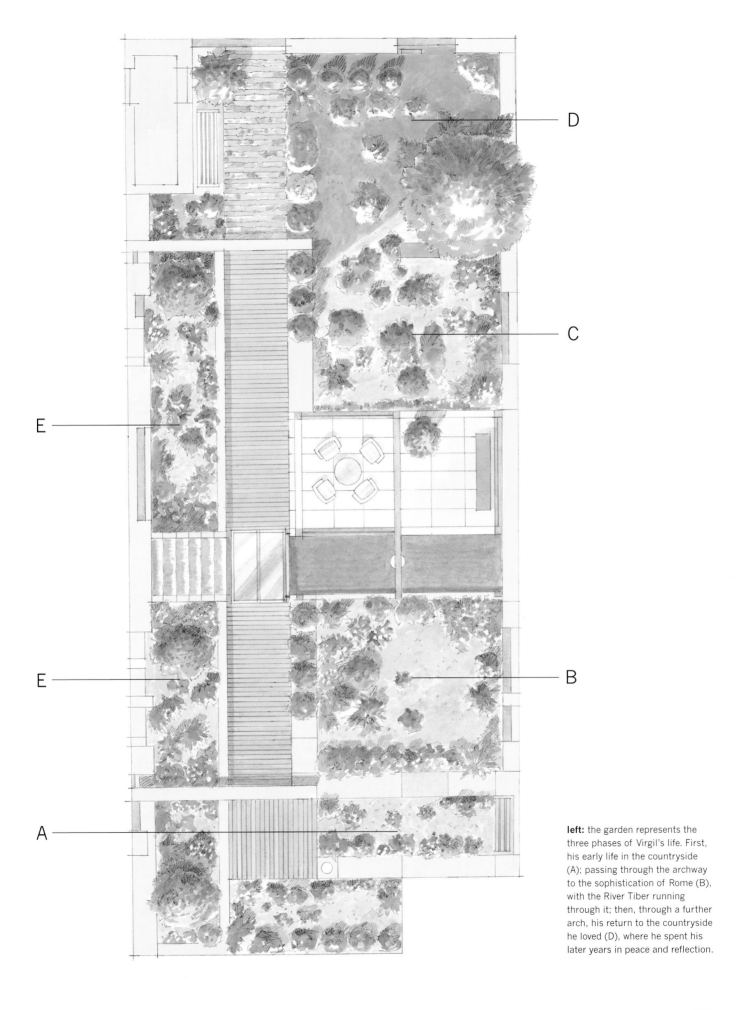

D

C

E

E

B

A

left: the garden represents the three phases of Virgil's life. First, his early life in the countryside (A); passing through the archway to the sophistication of Rome (B), with the River Tiber running through it; then, through a further arch, his return to the countryside he loved (D), where he spent his later years in peace and reflection.

the planting appears to be in a more open and relaxed 'meadow' style, as opposed to the closer and 'tighter' style of the traditional English border. Christopher admits to being very much inspired by a study tour in Europe, and in particular during a visit to the gardens and nurseries of Piet Oudolf, an exponent of the new movement, in Hummelo, the Netherlands. Piet kindly agreed to supply some of the plants, including astrantias and thalictrums, which were a key part of the overall planting scheme. The planting also takes in such rich floral colours as the mid and deep blues, deep pinks, wine reds and purples of the bearded irises, offset by touches of bright yellow as they rise above drifts of euphorbias: *E. dulcis* 'Chameleon', *E. cyparissias* 'Fens Ruby' and *E.* x *martinii*. In contrast to the spear-like leaves of the irises we have the velvety foliage of the phlomis, stachys and verbascum, punctuated by the striking exclamations of the silver-foliaged cardoon (*Cynara cardunculus*).

Moving on we pass under another square archway and enter into a more reflective area of the garden, the last phase of Virgil's life, when he returned to his beloved countryside to enjoy a period of wealth and well-being. Here the path changes from close-boarded decking to open strips of cedar. The limestone scree of the country reappears within a meadow-style planting, with its mixture of wildflowers and grasses.

The pathway terminates before a sculpted stone plaque, by Belinda Eade, which bears one of the many inscriptions that appear on walls throughout the

below: behind a planting of irises, alliums and *Acanthus spinosus*, the inscription reads: *But Rome carries her head as high above other cities as cypresses tower over the guelder rose.*

opposite: the timber decking, straight as a Roman road, with its glass bridge over the symbolic River Tiber, is shaded by an avenue of standard hornbeams.

below right: the urn and all the inscriptions were made by stone-carver Belinda Eade.

garden, taken from Virgil's *Eclogues*. Two thousand years on, as we enter the third millennium, this one seems especially pertinent: *Look at the cosmos trembling in its massive round, land and the expanse of ocean and the sky profound; look how they all are full of joy at the age to come…*

To one side of the plaque stand four pencil-thin sentinels of the Italian cypress (*Cupressus sempervirens*), while in a far corner stands a lone stone pine (*Pinus pinea*), all evoking the familiar image of the Italian landscape.

Christopher Bradley-Hole had been struck by the way that gardens in various periods of history, such as those of Renaissance Italy and of the 18th century in England, were often specifically designed to invoke moods, or to tell allegorical tales of romance or mythology. Here, he picks up the tradition of bringing allegory and narrative into the garden.

The overall success of this garden is to a major extent due to the skilful marriage of every element of the design. In a retrospective or informal garden one can often make adjustments as one goes, and a misaligned or crumbling wall can add charm. But here, the contemporary nature of the design and the materials used require precision and strict attention to detail to ensure that everything is in perfect alignment; to miss by an inch would be to miss by a mile.

Modern architecture is enjoying an exhilarating renaissance as we move into the new millennium, and the great challenge for garden designers is to look to the future and express new ideas. This garden is a part of that expression, and is a celebration of the designer and all the craftsmen who helped in its creation.

A ROMANTIC WOODLAND GARDEN

above: *Rosa* 'Parkdirektor Riggers' clothes the ruined tower in scarlet blooms. The crumbling wall is softened wih ferns (*Dryopteris filix-mas*) and the striking pure white spathes of the arum lily (*Zantedeschia aethiopica* 'Crowborough').

Some people believe that the natural-looking garden must be the easiest to create – after all, it is 'natural'. In fact, in many ways the opposite is true; it is far more difficult to achieve a truly natural look than a more formal mixture of hard and soft landscape. There is a fine line between a garden that simply feels abandoned and overrun and one that has atmosphere, an air of mystery and a special timeless quality.

This delightful woodland is such a garden. As the designer Arabella Lennox-Boyd says, 'It is as though you have slipped through a narrow gap in an old yew hedge and there you discover, to your surprise, an abandoned ruined stone tower upon a small island beside a stream and time, for a moment, stands still...'

The original inspiration came from Italy's gloriously romantic garden of Ninfa, near Rome, where gin-clear streams run between mediaeval ruins that are bedecked with a multitude of heavily scented roses. While there are elements of fantasy here, it is not too great a leap for the imagination to see how such a woodland garden could be created in any garden of reasonable size. It is also very much in the tradition of the folly, where extraordinary or deliberately ruined buildings were created within a particular setting to evoke a unique sense of place.

In this garden the ruined tower is the main focus and the stream acts as the link between the different elements. It runs around the island and under the turfed stone bridge that leads across to the gently rotting doorway in the old tower. It then winds its way down the length of the garden to finally disappear out of sight under a rustic bridge. Along its course are clumps of moisture-loving plants, the elegant pale blue *Iris sibirica* and pure white arum lilies contrasting with the rounded, deeply lobed leaves of *Gunnera tinctoria*, a smaller cousin of the giant *Gunnera manicata*.

Running up the banks on either side, the birch woodland is made up of a single variety, *Betula utilis*, the broken white colour of its bark contrasting with the dark understorey of *Quercus ilex* and *Osmanthus heterophyllus*, both of which help to blend out the boundary. In the foreground a complementary mix of *Spiraea* X *vanhouttei* and *Viburnum opulus* 'Roseum' is punctuated with drifts of white foxgloves.

Beneath the birches the grassy banks are interspersed with a naturalized woodland mixture of cranesbills, Solomon's seal, periwinkle and ferns, along with a tangled mass of white rambling roses.

So often today, gardens seem to be over-designed and over-stocked, full of man-made articles: paving, furniture and objets d'art. Sometimes it is pleasing simply to work with nature and with a light touch to create a feeling of timeless peace and harmony. Looking at this garden, it is quite extraordinary to know that it was all created from nothing in just two weeks.

If you're wondering how the tower was built in such a short time along with everything else – it was constructed, off site, in such a way that it could be taken apart, transported to the show, and re-assembled like a giant jigsaw puzzle!

above: beyond the bold foliage of *Gunnera tinctoria*, the white rambling rose *Rosa* 'Seagull' tumbles down to the stream.
below: viewed from the timber decking on the right, the eye follows the stream to the old stone tower and its arched bridge.

SCULPTURE IN THE GARDEN

Here we have a garden whose concept is essentially based on the formal setting of the sculpture gardens of the 17th century, but which has been reinterpreted in the contemporary manner of today. The designer George Carter feels that the Baroque gardens of that time are surprisingly closer to modern minimalist designs than the more 'naturalistic' gardens of the 18th and 19th centuries. All the elements of the classic late 17th-century gardens are used here – water, topiary, architecture and sculpture – and arranged to create an outdoor gallery with a series of exciting vistas.

The designer also drew inspiration from earlier periods, such as that of the Italian Renaissance, when sculpture played an important role in many gardens. Around 1505, Pope Julius II commissioned the great architect and artist Bramante to draw up a plan to link the papal palace in the Vatican with the Villa Belvedere, an earlier Pope's country house. Bramante's design for the Cortile di Belvedere was a remarkable architectural achievement, and this vast garden included an open-air sculpture gallery, containing many great works of art, both contemporary and from antiquity.

And, going back even further, there were similar examples in the time of the Roman Empire, in particular the great garden surrounding Emperor Hadrian's villa at Tivoli. Many pieces were set among colonnades, grottoes and walks, not simply as objets d'art but as an integral part of the overall design.

This garden is laid out on a long rectangle and viewed from the front and down one side. Rather than using colour and masses of planting, it relies on the simple play of light against dark foliage, on water, and on contrasting textures. There are three main axes delineated by three canals, the widest running down the centre, with one on either side. The canals are shallow, black-lined and edged with polished steel, giving an overall sense of stillness and a reflected air of tranquillity.

The foreground of grey and silver foliage is studded with topiary forms, in particular the conical pyramids of *Phillyrea angustifolia* – once the most favoured of all plants for topiary but now virtually unused. They rise up from mats of *Nepeta* 'Six Hills Giant', *Artemisia* 'Powis Castle' and *Stachys byzantina*, with massed clumps of rosemary *(Rosmarinus officinalis)*, *Santolina chamaecyparissus* 'Lambrook Silver' and *Helichrysum splendidum* lying at the centre. Running around the edges, the lacy leaves of *Senecio cineraria* contrast with spiky clumps of *Festuca glauca*.

Beyond this, mid-way along the length of the canals, a group of eight plane trees *(Platanus acerifolia)* have been planted in pairs. They have been trained into tall flat umbrellas to provide a ceiling of foliage and dappled light over the pair of highly polished aluminium sculptures – collectively entitled The Hyaline – by Georgina Miller. The sculptures are placed, partly submerged, in the two outer canals, each giving a mirror image in the still waters.

The sections leading up to the final sculptures are very simple, with the vertical forms of the yew topiary cones rising from the horizontal plane of the close-clipped turf. This extends to the dark bluish green, rusticated façade, behind which stand five sentinels of Italian cypresses *(Cupressus sempervirens* 'Stricta'). The architectural façade provides the perfect frame for the three focal elements of sculpture lying at the head of each of the canals.

In the centre, the splendid form of The Calydonian Boar, by Neil Simmons, sits back on his haunches, in reflective mood upon his island plinth. On either side, in their separate niches, are bronze masks by the sculptor Olivia Musgrave. To the right, Orpheus mourns the loss of his beloved Eurydice; to the left, Apollo and Daphne are locked in eternal torment by Cupid's cruel arrows. Both pieces are elevated upon pedestals that rise out of the waters of the canal.

Viewed from the front, the garden is seen through the frame of four tall, rusticated piers; their air of solid permanence is deceptive, since they are actually made of wood, painted in matt grey. Each one carries a gilded or silvered sphere, designed by George Carter, with emblematic detail symbolic of the weather: Sun, Rain, Lightning and Frost. Viewed from the side, across the canals, the long boundary is delineated by a trellis screen backed with sheets of polished galvanized steel. This creates a diffused reflective image that helps to dissolve the boundary; this was selected in preference to the clear image that would have resulted if mirror glass had been used.

Here we have a garden full of classic grace and style and yet, at the same time, a garden where the designer has put the unmistakable stamp of our time upon it, both in terms of the materials used and in the ways in which they have been used. The result is a serene and reflective setting for the sculptural pieces.

A different approach to garden layout and planting may be more suited to other styles of sculpture. A naturalistic setting would be appropriate for a life-like animal figure; a planting using bold colour or form would set off a simple or abstract piece; the introduction of an unexpected element in the planting – or alternatively a massed single variety – would be the ideal backdrop to a whimsical or surreal sculpture.

The creation of a garden is itself an art form, but one that inevitably changes with the seasons and evolves with time; the inclusion of sculpture brings an extra dimension, and a note of permanence.

above and opposite: bronze heads of Orpheus (above) and Daphne and Apollo (opposite) were clearly inspired by Greek mythology. The inspiration for the chrome-plated aluminium pieces partly submerged in the canals was the artist's scuba-diving trip to the Red Sea.

THE QUARRYMAN'S GARDEN

This garden is about conservation, in particular the conservation of butterflies. It incorporates a variety of habitats in order to explore the possibilities of creating a garden that is both beautiful and ideal for wildlife. Undoubtedly, wild gardens are among the most difficult to get right; this is especially true of show gardens, when they must be completed in just two weeks. The skill lies in achieving the magical touch that you know is present when you hear the comment 'It looks as if it's always been there.' Gardens like these are rarely drawn up in detail; a sketch may be made of the overall concept, but it is only on site that the different elements are brought together by those involved in its creation.

Marney Hall, ecologist and wild plant expert, joined up with Paul Dyer, who specializes in creating 'natural' water features; they combined their respective talents to bring about a wild garden that really does look as though it has been there for ever. It is a skill that requires a good eye for colour and form and also a certain humility to respect and observe just how Mother Nature works when left to her own devices.

This garden is based on a simple story. Mr Machaon is a retired quarry owner who lives on the edge of an old limestone quarry, some of which is now disused and overgrown. All his life he has had a passion for butterflies, and he has observed how, once old workings are abandoned, wildlife – especially butter-flies – quickly moves in.

The garden is Mr Machaon's personal nature reserve, in which he has tried to work with nature rather than against it, creating in the process something that is very special to him. Each day he walks the worn pathway between the rocks at the top of the quarry, through a colourful array of wild flowers that have made themselves at home among the rocks: wild thyme, horseshoe vetch, birdsfoot trefoil, rock rose and sheepsbit. His path follows a cornfield, the corner of which he has persuaded the farmer to leave unsprayed. This encourages the butterflies and birds that feed and breed on such plants as the cornflowers and corn marigolds that survive around the field's edges.

Towards the end of the field is an old fence and stile, which takes him beside Speckled Wood. The ancient trees were felled some 25 years ago and only the stumps remain, but the naturally regenerating trees suggest what was originally there: oak, chestnut, hazel and ash. Within the wood, a spring bubbles out of the ground, forming a stream that runs alongside his cabin, tumbling over the rocks between a profusion of wild and cultivated flowers. Fragrant drifts of the violet-purple sweet rocket run through the pinky-mauve and bluey-white stars of osteospermum; clumps of red valerian, with its tiny, pinky-red flowers, pick up the bluish-purple and mini red-hot poker tips of *Primula vialii*.

Mr Machaon's pride and joy is the old timber cabin, inspired by one he had seen long ago on a trip to the Adirondack Mountains in America. It has been

opposite: surrounding the cabin, a great variety of nectar-rich flowers create an inviting habitat for butterflies.
below left: the gate posts are made from a single piece of stone, split to reveal two halves of an ammonite.
below: foxgloves, sweet rocket and scabious flourish beside the stream.

lovingly built from pieces of wood and windows that he has collected over time. Its design was a challenge to his ingenuity and has allowed him to indulge his hobby of woodcarving. It was in fact designed and created by Philip Game, artist and passionate builder of 'follies', and David Williams, artist, furniture maker and wood carver. Together they assembled an assortment of items, ranging from the flooring from an old scout hut, paint-peeling bargeboards from a village shop, oak-bark tiles, driftwood trunks from the banks of the River Wye and an abandoned spindleback chair from a friend's garage…all in all, it is a triumphant tribute to the art of recycling.

Mr Machaon has worked hard to convince his neighbours of the importance of respecting the environment. Many species of butterfly will feed and breed in our gardens if the right combination of foodplants, sunshine and shelter is present. He insists that, like his, every garden can, in its own way, be a nature reserve.

Why Mr Machaon? Marney Hall has been studying butterflies for more than 25 years and her favourite is the Swallowtail, *Papilio machaon*.

opposite: this striking blend of wild and cultivated flowers includes the blue ceanothus, purple heliotrope, *Scabious* 'Butterfly Blue', the lilac *Phlox* 'Scented Pillow' and *Alyssum* 'Little Dorrit'. Splashes of yellow appear on the wild pansy or heartsease (*Viola tricolor*), supported by the wallflower (*Erysimum* 'Bowles' Yellow') and the yellow flag iris (*Iris pseudacorus*).

Trees
Ash
Aspen
Field maple
Lime
Oak
Wild cherry
Willow

Woodland plants
Bluebell
Cow parsley
Female fern
Foxglove
Great woodrush
Greater stitchwort
Hedge garlic
Lady's slipper orchid
Lily of the valley
Male fern
Nettle
Nettle-leaved bellflower
Peach-leaved bellflower
Ostrich fern
Primrose
Red campion
Solomon's seal
Sweet violet
Teasel
White campion
Wood spurge

Shrubs
Blackthorn

Buckthorn
Crab apple
Gorse
Hawthorn
Hazel
Holly
Honeysuckle
Ivy
Privet
Rosa 'Kent'
Rosa filipes 'Kiftsgate'
Rosa 'Rambling Rector'
Rosa 'Seagull'
Spindle

Meadow plants
Broad-leaved dock
Buttercup
Common catsear
Cowslip
Daisy
Fritillary
Germander speedwell
Marjoram
Meadow saxifrage
Meadow vetchling
Mouse-ear hawkweed
Ox-eye daisy
Quaking grass
Ragged robin
Red clover
Ribswort plantain
Salad burnet
Selfheal

Silverweed
Southern marsh orchid
Spear thistle
Spotted orchid
Sorrel

Rock plants
Birdsfoot trefoil
Black spleenwort
Burdock
Dickies fern
Harebell
Hart's-tongue fern
Heartsease
Herb Robert
Horseshoe vetch
Kidney vetch
Ivy-leaved toadflax
Maidenhair spleenwort
Mullein
Pyramid orchid
Rock rose
Sea campion
Sheepsbit
Stonecrop
Thrift
Weld
Wild strawberry
Wild thyme

Wetland plants
Bugle
Creeping Jenny
Great water dock

Kingcup
Milk parsley
Mimulus
Royal fern
Soft rush
Water forget-me-not
Water mint
Yellow flag

Border plants
Ageratum
Alyssum
Broom
Buddleia
Ceanothus
Cistus
Erigeron
Escallonia
Hebe
Heliotrope
Honesty
Lavender
Lilac
Milk thistle
Osteospermum
Phlox
Potentilla
Red valerian
Runner beans
Scabious
Sedum
Sweet rocket
Wallflower

A WATER MEADOW GARDEN

above: pollarded willows leaning away from the prevailing winds create a strong sense of being in an open, somewhat windswept landscape.

opposite: the ceramic poles seem to arise naturally from the reed beds. Their colour and form capture the three key elements of the water meadow: the horizontal landscape, the vertical vegetation and the movement of fish.

Here the designer Mark Anthony Walker demonstrates how it is possible to take a perfectly natural setting, such as a fenland water meadow, and by the simple introduction of two man-made elements, to create a unique sense of place; a natural garden in a natural setting.

The corner of a much larger meadow has been 'lifted up' and placed on the site, with the tree-lines, water-way and decking set off at a slight angle to the site's boundaries. This in a subtle way creates 'movement' and leads the eye to believe that each extends beyond the site. To have set them square on would have led to a visually static feeling, giving the overall sense that the whole piece was self-contained and complete.

Around the boundary, on two sides, willow withies (*Salix caladendron*) are planted to give a seamless edge, blending into the countryside beyond. Five pollarded willows (*Salix alba*) create the framework, their windswept, gnarled and fissured trunks all just slightly leaning away from the prevailing force.

Running around the water's edge, beneath the willows, the meadow grassland is full of indigenous flowering varieties such as angelica (*Angelica archangelica*), ragged robin (*Lychnis flos-cuculi*), buttercups (*Ranunculus lingua*) and snake's head fritillary (*Fritillaria meleagris*), along with marginals of bogbean (*Menyanthes trifoliata*), marsh marigolds (*Caltha palustris*), water forget-me-not (*Myosotis scorpioides*), flag iris *(Iris pseudacorus)* and small clumps of pure white arum lilies (*Zantedeschia aethiopica*).

In the foreground, a mass planting of reed and sedge is interspersed with ceramic poles by the artist Jonathan Keep. The colour and forms of the poles, with their abstracted fish shapes, reflect in the water and perfectly complement the russet colours of the swaying reeds. Because of its open style, you are able to 'view through' the sculpture to the willows and beyond.

The simple decking of reeded timber seems almost to float out over the water and allows you to walk right into the heart of the garden, where you can observe at close quarters the abundance of aquatic life. All these subtle elements combine to provide a quiet retreat, where you might unfold your canvas chair on a balmy summer's day and quietly contemplate the gentle sights and sounds of nature; the sudden iridescent flash of a dragonfly's wings and the fluffy black down of baby moorhens busily threading between the reeds.

A GARDEN FOR CHILDREN

above: Ratty's riverside house, with its turfed roof, is the charming centrepiece of this imaginative garden.

This is a garden to delight children and adults alike. It takes us into the wonderful fantasy world of Ratty's river bank in Kenneth Grahame's classic children's book, *The Wind in the Willows*. The designer Bunny Guinness has succeeded in moving right away from the standard play garden with its plastic slide, climbing frame and sandpit. She wanted to introduce children to the pleasures of simple gardening and wildlife and to allow them the irresistible joy of playing with and around water.

At the very heart of the garden is Ratty's beautifully crafted riverside house, complete with veranda and mooring post for his little row boat, ready and waiting with its overflowing picnic basket. What child would not be delighted to have such a playhouse? Certainly different to the average 'Wendy house' that usually resembles a miniature garden shed with curtains, here we have a little abode full of character and fun features such as the ladder that allows you to climb up inside the chimney and out onto the turf roof, with its fringe of the common hop (*Humulus lupulus*) running along the front edge.

With two children of her own, Bunny Guinness is keenly aware of safety issues. Throughout the garden, care has been taken to ensure that it is a safe place in which to play, especially with regard to the various water features. There is a metal grid just below the surface of the deeper water in front of the landing deck, then the water cascades down to a shallow stream no more than 50mm (2 inches) deep, trickling over pebbles set in mortar and ending in a pool with its own beach for sand play. This section has been constructed so that it can be drained down for periodic cleaning.

The informal style of planting along the water's edge – using a selection of waterside and marginal plants – creates a very natural feel. Following the stream are descending clumps of *Ligularia dentata* 'Desdemona', its heart-shaped leaves suffused with dark purplish-bronze forming a perfect foil to the bright orange flowers that appear in midsummer, in contrast to the purple-blue heads of the spiky-leaved *Iris sibirica*. In the deeper water are water lilies and the highly fragrant, forked white flowers of the Cape pondweed (*Aponogeton distachyos*). Edging the upper pool, the flowering rush (*Butomus umbellatus*) has delicate rose-pink umbels; pale blue forget-me-not flowers of *Myosotis scorpioides* 'Mermaid' run around its feet, and spiky sprays of *Typha minima* pierce the surface of the water. On the bank the young leaves of the giant gunnera (*Gunnera manicata*) are starting to grow among arching sprays of the white bell flowers of Solomon's seal (*Polygonatum* x *hybridum*) and nestling clumps of the early-flowering, pink, locket-like flowers of bleeding heart (*Dicentra spectabilis*).

below: an ancient, hollow willow tree, given a door, becomes a secret den.

Mixed shrub and herbaceous		Marginal and water plants	Cottage and vegetable garden
Acanthus mollis	*Hesperis matronalis*	*Aponogeton distachyos*	
Aegopodium podagraria	*Humulus lupulus*	*Butomus umbellatus*	*Anthemis tinctoria* 'E C Buxton'
'Variegatum'	*Iris foetidissima* 'Variegata'	*Caltha palustris*	*Buxus sempervirens* 'Suffruticosa'
Agapanthus Headbourne Hybrids	*Lonicera* x *brownii* 'Dropmore	*Darmera peltata*	*Helianthus annuus*
Ajuga reptans 'Catlin's Giant'	Scarlet'	*Glyceria maxima* var. *variegata*	*Matthiola incana* 'Cinderella
Angelica archangelica	*Lunaria annua* 'Alba Variegata'	*Gunnera manicata*	Series'
Arundo donax 'Variegata'	*Mahonia lomariifolia*	*Iris sibirica*	*Nicotiana* sp.
Asplenium scolopendrium	*Melianthus major*	*Ligularia dentata* 'Desdemona'	*Petunia* 'Dark Blue Frenzy'
Aucuba japonica	*Miscanthus sinensis* 'Zebrinus'	*Lysichiton americanus*	*Petunia* 'Express Sky Blue'
Bamboos – variegated	*Omphalodes verna*	*Lysimachia nummularia* 'Aurea'	*Salvia patens* 'Cambridge Blue'
Brunnera macrophylla	*Osmanthus heterophyllus*	*Menyanthes trifoliata*	*Soleirolia soleirolii*
Brunnera macrophylla 'Hadspen	*Osmunda regalis*	*Myosotis scorpioides*	*Viola* sp.
Cream'	*Persicaria bistorta* 'Superba'	*Nuphar lutea*	
Campanula persicifolia	*Pittosporum tobira*	*Nymphoides peltata*	Chives
Centranthus ruber	*Polygonatum* x *hybridum*	*Phalaris arundinacea* var. *picta*	Climbing golden French beans
Centranthus ruber 'Albus'	*Primula florindae*	*Potamogeton crispus*	Courgettes
Crinodendron hookerianum	*Pseudosasa japonica*	*Ranunculus lingua*	Leeks
Dicentra spectabilis	*Pulmonaria rubra*	*Rheum palmatum*	Ornamental cabbage
Digitalis purpurea	*Rosa* 'Arctic Snow'	*Typha latifolia*	Red onion
Dipsacus fullonum	*Symphytum* x *uplandicum*	*Typha minima*	Red chard
Fargesia murieliae	'Variegatum'		Strawberry spinach
Ferns – various	*Trollius* x *cultorum* 'Superbus'		Sweetcorn
Griselinia littoralis	*Verbascum bombyciferum*		Tomatoes
Hedera helix	*Zantedeschia aethiopica*		Yellow squash

opposite: surrounded by the wild flowers of the meadow, Ratty takes a nap under the old apple tree, up which clambers the honeysuckle (*Lonicera* x *brownii* 'Dropmore Scarlet').

The broad timbered bridge takes us past a gnarled and hollow willow tree, with its cranky old doorway adding an air of mystery and intrigue. The cut log pathway leads up to a small vegetable patch alongside Ratty's rooftop, with sunflowers and neat clipped box hedging enclosing beds of runner beans, courgettes, tomatoes and sweetcorn. What better way to introduce children to gardening, than through growing and nurturing vegetables that they will ultimately be able to eat freshly picked?

Within this garden is a great abundance of mixed planting to excite and stimulate. A sturdy framework is provided by tougher, more child-resistant plants such as clumps of hazel (*Corylus avellana*) and willows (*Salix alba* 'Vitellina' and *Salix elaeagnos*), along with an elegant, fast-growing waterside tree, the common alder (*Alnus glutinosa*); in spring this has the added attraction of clusters of long, dark brown catkins.

Drifts of herbaceous plants add splashes of colour. Heavily scented stocks and nicotiana in pastel and primary shades mingle with the tall stems of *Verbascum bombyciferum*, whose grey, felted leaves provide a perfect backcloth for the reddish-pink, star-like flowers of the red valerian (*Centranthus rubur*) and the purple frills of the decorative cabbages. A mass of soft pink flowers of *Persicaria bistorta* 'Superba' tumbles down to the edge of the sandy bank along with clumps of trollius, with their cool lemon flowers.

At the front of the garden there is an open area of meadow grass dotted with wild flowers – primulas, cowslips, ragged robin and the sparkling moon daisies – running down to the water's edge, where stands of fresh green ferns, including *Dryopteris filix-mas*, and candelabra primula rise above a tangle of mixed ivies and *Ajuga reptans* 'Catlin's Giant'.

At the centre of the meadow is an old apple tree with a simple swing hanging from one of its craggy boughs. There, lying back and savouring the sweet smell of the meadow grasses, is Ratty himself. Nearby, sitting on the bankside with his toes in the stream, is the handsome Mr Toad, resplendent in blazer, dicky-bow and straw boater. These charming creatures were meticulously crafted by John Carnell, of Torbay Borough Council in Devon. They are constructed over a framework of fine steel bars and chicken wire, which is filled with a moist retentive soil mix. Succulents are individually planted through the mesh, each variety carefully selected to give the required texture and colour.

Whether built as a secluded corner in a much larger garden or as a self-sufficient 'wild' garden, this is the sort of garden that would evolve into a magical place to provide endless hours of pleasure for all the family.

opposite: the vegetable garden is certainly not all about greens – there are golden beans, purple-blue cabbages and the pink flowers of chives.
below: with a sandy beach just a short hop away from a grassy meadow, what more could any child want?

THE RAILWAY GARDEN

opposite: the broken-down area of the platform cleverly introduces a water feature ...a cascade down the steps, across the paving and over the edge to the bog garden among the railway tracks.

Here we have the ultimate dream garden for those who want to travel back in time to the romantic age of steam. For sheer nostalgia this garden could scarcely be bettered, whether for reawakening personal reminiscences or evoking the romance of the silver screen: *Brief Encounters* with Trevor Howard and Celia Johnson; Alec Guinness and Peter Sellers in *The Lady Killers*; Richard Rodney Bennett's music playing over the opening scene of *Murder on the Orient Express*, as the train gathers speed and pulls out of old Istanbul. Or remember the rhythmic pace of W H Auden's voice – 'This is the night mail crossing the border, Bringing the cheque and the postal order, Letters for the rich, letters for the poor, the shop at the corner, the girl next door…' – or the recordings of those mighty steam locomotives 'The Great Western' and 'The Flying Scotsman' – or that once-familiar sound of the branch line train chugging into the station, hissing steam, coming to a stop and then the evocative opening click and dull clunk of the closing carriage doors. Well, maybe we are getting a little carried away, but there is no reason why today's technology cannot support yesterday's memories: you simply wire the garden for sound…

Whether or not you wish to travel down memory lane, the design of this garden lends itself perfectly to the juxtaposition of naturalistic and cultivated styles of planting. The late Geoff Hamilton felt that it showed how, in a relatively small space, you could create a number of distinct areas, each with their own character, and yet retain an overall feeling of harmony, each part complementing the other. The original inspiration for the garden came from an area in north Wales that the designer, Julian Dowle, often visits with his wife. They stay in a cottage within sight of Snowdon and nearby is an abandoned railway, much of which has been left to nature. This **gave** him the idea of creating a garden that combined the subtle blend of the 'natural' with the cultivated.

At the lowest level, in the foreground, the broken-up section of the old railway track is the obvious home to a completely natural style of planting. Stunted silver birch and willows, buttercups and daisies, wild roses, foxgloves, willow herb and cow parsley sprout up between and alongside the sleepers – very much as we can see along any disused siding glimpsed from a train window.

The next level up is the paved terrace of the semi-derelict platform, with its slatted timber bench seat. Here we see the clever introduction of water: a spring

rising on the upper level cascades down the steps and runs across the broken sections of paving and on over the edge of the platform to create a small water-fall. Down at track level the water forms a pond, an ideal habitat for frogs and newts, with its waterside planting of yellow flag irises and common mallow. A small pump, hidden in a sump beneath one of the railway sleepers, recirculates the water to the top of the steps.

Behind the platform, raised on a Cotswold dry-stone wall, is a cottage garden with its riot of colourful planting: irises, foxgloves, lupins and aquilegias, with saxifrage, phlox, helianthemum and *Geum* 'Mrs Bradshaw' tumbling down over the wall. Beyond the flowers a wire strand fence is almost hidden by espaliered fruit trees and old-fashioned blackberries. In the corner is the old Booking Office – now serving as the garden shed – with its vegetable garden running off to one side, enclosed by a white-painted picket fence.

To ensure that the old station felt authentic in every way, it was essential to use genuine artefacts from the past. Julian worked closely with two steam con-servation groups: The Dean Forest Railway Society and The Gloucestershire & Warwickshire Railway Society. Both had, for many years, been active in the ren-ovation of old steam trains and branch lines that, in the 1960s, had fallen foul of

Dr Beeching and his cruel cuts. The societies were able to loan special items such as the milk churns, waiting for the early morning 'milk train'; the old station bench with its cast-iron base embossed with the Gloucestershire & Warwickshire initials; the Victorian station lampposts with their stirrup lanterns; and of course the Booking Office, painted in chocolate brown and cream, the line colours of the Dean Forest Railway Company. The final result is truly that of a station where time has stood still. So real was the overall effect of the garden, so powerful the memories evoked, that a number of people stood before it with tears running down their cheeks.

However, there were a number of disasters along the way. Because the general construction is done with a weak mix to allow for easy demolition, and because there was an extraordinary amount of rain during the build-up period, a crack appeared in the platform retaining wall, which, although small to begin with, grew larger each day. Fortunately it lasted to the end of the week and actually added something to the overall feeling of abandoned dereliction! And then, while dismantling the garden, a fork-lift truck driver dropped the Booking Office, reducing it to a flat-pack! The aforementioned Society was not amused; they sent a hefty bill to have it restored to the original state in which they had supplied it.

below: down on the railway track sits an old wooden trolley, now overgrown with alder, foxgloves, cow parsley and ragged robin.

COUNTRY LIFE CENTENARY GARDEN

above: curly-coated wirework sheep in a colourful setting planted by wildflower specialist Marney Hall.

The grounds of a fine old country house with its adjacent parkland provide the imagined setting for this garden, created to celebrate the centenary of *Country Life* magazine. The designer Rupert Golby called on a number of artists and craftsmen and women to ensure that the garden captured the spirit of the magazine which, for 100 years, has portrayed and applauded the finest manifestations of architecture, fine art, gardening, farming, wildlife, and the arts and crafts of the countryside.

In the foreground is the intimate, sunken courtyard garden with the central feature of a raised brick, quatrefoil pool with cut stone coping. At the centre of the pool is a polished bronze fountain, created by Simon Allison, with a horizontal disc of clear glass creating a curtain of water through which you glimpse the swimming and leaping bronze trout. Around the pool is raked gravel with a light scattering of ornamental grasses and free-seeding and creeping plants such as *Sisyrinchium striatum* and *Erigeron karvinskianus.*

Rising up on three sides, brick retaining walls support borders of mixed planting with matching brick paving leading around the perimeter at the upper level. Throughout this area of planting the dominant colours are across the spectrum of purples and blues, offset with glaucous and grey foliage and highlighted by many varieties of white roses. Blue delphiniums are set against the

smoky foliage of *Salix purpurea* 'Nancy Saunders'. The striking purple spikes of the wallflower *Erysimum* 'Bowles' Mauve' contrast with the silvery, wiry *Corokia* x *virgata*. The purple-leaved, cerise-petalled *Rosa glauca* harmonizes in colour, but not in form, with the *Allium hollandicum* 'Purple Sensation'. Domes of lavender punctuate the pathways, their aromatic scent mingling with the heady perfume of the regal lilies and white shrub roses. Swathes of pale lilac geraniums are peppered with brilliant flowering opium poppies. Tall slender stems of pale blue flag irises rise above drifts of the catmint *Nepeta* 'Six Hills Giant'. The lilac sweet rocket (*Hesperis matronalis*) blends with the misty foliage of the bronze fennel in strong contrast to the bold form of *Melianthus major* and the architectural angelica, with its towering umbels.

In addition to the central fountain in this part of the garden, two other features were commissioned to demonstrate the magazine's ongoing support for present-day artists. Set above the planting at the front of the garden are a pair of beautifully crafted bronze urns by the sculptor William Fawke. Based on the idea of enfolding butterfly wings, the iridescent verdigris and bronze colouring complements the planting beyond. Midway along the boundary wall, within a niche, there sits a transparent, lifesize, blown glass figure by the sculptor Johannes von Stumm. The figure has an eerie, almost ghost-like presence, a

above: drawing on the past, the garden makes considerable use of reclaimed materials, such as the paving stones and genuine Tudor bricks. The arts and crafts of the present day are also strongly supported: the fountain's splendidly original design includes leaping bronze trout – cast from real fish.

feeling that is endorsed by the sculptor's comment: 'I wanted to make a figure of contemplation, which just sits and observes...'

Beyond the central area, a wide flight of York stone steps leads up to a pair of magnificent wrought iron gates, topped with an ornately scrolled pediment with the 'CL' monogram; these were built by the artist-blacksmith Richard Quinnell. The gates are carried on piers of brick and dressed Cotswold stone and surmounted by seated cherubs of cast lead. Jade oil was applied to give the cherubs an aged patination.

Flanking the gates are a pair of exquisitely detailed brick and stone Hidcote-style pavilions with swept pitched roofs of Cotswold stone tiles. They were designed by Rupert Golby with help from the architect John Simpson. The bricks used for the pavilions and elsewhere in the garden are especially interesting: they are hand-made genuine Tudor bricks rescued from a collapsed barn.

The commitment to every aspect of design is further demonstrated by the interior of the outer pavilion. It is decorated as a garden study, with Georgian-style plasterwork by Ian Constantinides and trompe l'oeil ceiling paintings by Simon Brady. It is furnished with antique furniture and a pair of obelisk bookcases made by Christopher Clark, and filled with paintings and small items of sculpture from the Hiscox Collection, including works by Henry Moore, Walter Sickert, Barbara Hepworth and Mark Gertler. And to complete the study, there is a portrait of Edward Hudson, the founder of *Country Life*, together with his original office chair, designed by his contemporary and friend, Sir Edwin Lutyens. Needless to say the pavilion was securely alarmed and the works of art were removed at night to a large safe in the other pavilion.

Beyond the main garden, through the iron gates, we glimpse a timeless scene of pastoral serenity. The extraordinarily lifelike wirework sheep, made by sculptor Rupert Till, graze contentedly in a lush meadow of wildflowers planted out by the ecologist and designer Marney Hall. Here we have buttercups, ox-eye daisies, cowslips and ragged robins, with flag iris and burr rush in the boggy area by the ancient uprooted oak.

To complete the scene behind the pavilion there is a sheep's shelter. Master thatchers Parkinson Blackwell left the long straw to age in an open barn for over a year in order to achieve a truly dilapidated, rustic look. Just one more instance of the superb eye for detail that is present throughout this splendid example of the creative art of gardening.

above: irises, alliums, roses, sweet rocket and vivid blue cornflowers combine in this glorious planting.
left: the delicacy of a butterfly's wing is captured in this bronze urn, framed by the young stems of teasels, lupins, foxgloves and the fragrant honeysuckle *Lonicera* x *americana*.

AN ENGLISH COUNTRY GARDEN

This is a garden of simplicity and harmony that combines a sense of space with a feeling of enclosed tranquillity. Italian-born Arabella Lennox-Boyd confesses to having a long love affair with English gardens throughout her years as a designer; here she shows how the two cultural threads entwine, with the softness of the English planting and the strong architectural style reminiscent of the classic gardens of the Italian Renaissance.

The overall plan is deceptively simple. A slightly raised L-shaped terrace overlooks a lower central area surrounded by herbaceous borders, all enclosed by high hedges of clipped yew. It would work equally well as the garden of a town house or as part of a large country garden.

The terrace area is kept deliberately plain and open, with a timber balustrade painted deep olive to match the beautiful open-sided timber pavilion at one end, with its slatted roof draped in quilted fabric. This was inspired by an early photograph showing the designer's mother seated beneath a similar garden pavilion overlooking Lake Como in northern Italy. All the timber work was crafted by Melvyn Heath, a near neighbour of Arabella's in Lancashire, and clearly demonstrates the joinery skill that is so necessary to ensure the quality of architectural or ornamental features within a garden.

The brick paving – in the palest terracotta – is laid in a basket weave pattern and provides the link from the terrace down the steps to the pathway. This takes you around the central feature of the three-tiered ziggurat of clipped box and then on to the focal point of the yew hedge, clipped to form a classical pediment held aloft by two squared columns. Between the columns a 'dark' opening leads off to left or right; either to another part of a larger garden or simply to out-of-sight utility areas.

left: this beautifully proportioned garden combines luscious herbaceous borders with the geometric shapes of the various archictectural features: the octagonal pavilion, the central ziggurat of clipped box and the imposing yew pediment.

The colour of the paving acts as a low-key foil to the herbaceous borders in myriad subtle colours. There is just a touch of formality, with the round balls of clipped box backed by spiky sprays of variegated hostas set at each corner of the central square. But elsewhere the style is that of bountiful abundance. A selection of shrubs forms the basic framework of the deep borders. The variegated leaves of the cornus and the creamy white of the *Buddleja davidii* 'Harlequin' provide areas of lightness that are picked up by the fragrant groups of floribunda roses: the ice white of *Rosa* 'Iceberg' and the pearly white of *Rosa* 'Margaret Merril'. The herbaceous plants are massed in clumps rising up from the front of the border; the vibrant purples of *Allium* 'Purple Sensation' and the fluffy lilac-purple of *Thalictrum aquilegiifolium* contrast with the sparkling highlights of white lupins and sweet rocket. Even more intense points of interest are added by the deep crimson-maroon of the Gallica rose 'Tuscany Superb' and the striking forms of *Acanthus spinosus* and the purple-mauve cardoon thistle.

Much of the planting was supplied by the nurseryman John Metcalf, who caused quite a stir among the judges by so wonderfully demonstrating how it is possible to plant a show garden in a more 'natural' manner; where there are plants just coming into flower, in full flower or just going over. The tendency at the Chelsea Flower Show is to have everything at its biggest and best, in full bloom, even if plants have to be forced – or held back – to perform on schedule. John also feels that to value herbaceous plants for their flowers alone does them an injustice. 'We should also enjoy their foliage, which after all is there for six or seven months, whereas the flower may only be there for three or four weeks...'

The planting is set off to perfection by the dark backdrop of the high yew hedges. But these presented one of the greatest challenges of the whole garden. It would have been impossible to form 'instant' hedges with naturally grown yew. Again John Metcalf was able to help, having had experience of working as a television scenic artist. Sections of timber framework were made up to the exact profile of hedging and covered with fine chicken wire. It was then the lot of one of John's colleagues to take thousands of cuttings from mature yew hedges and to spend two weeks laboriously feeding them through the wire. The 'hedges' were then sprayed with a retarder and transported to site. It was feared that the whole thing might gently turn brown, but apart from the occasional touch-up with green paint it worked perfectly, and you can't see the joins!

above: the pink-purples of *Allium hollandicum* 'Purple Sensation' *Aethionema* 'Warley Rose' and *Geranium cinereum* 'Ballerina' lift the whole border.
opposite: the timber pavilion offers a vantage point from which to admire the beauty of the abundant borders.

Acanthus spinosus
Aethionema 'Warley Rose'
Alchemilla mollis
Allium aflatunense
Allium hollandicum 'Purple Sensation'
Anchusa azurea 'Loddon Royalist'
Anthemis punctata subsp. *cupaniana*
Artemisia 'Powis Castle'
Aster tongolensis 'Lavender Star'
Campanula persicifolia 'Hampstead White'
Chaerophyllum hirsutum 'Roseum'
Cornus alba 'Elegantissima'
Cynara cardunculus
Delphinium 'Blue Fountains'

Dianthus 'Maggie'
Dictamnus albus
Epimedium x *rubrum*
Filipendula rubra 'Venusta Magnifica'
Foeniculum vulgare 'Giant Bronze'
Galactites tomentosa
Geranium cinereum 'Ballerina'
Geranium 'Johnson's Blue'
Geranium pratense 'Mrs Kendall Clark'
Geranium psilostemon
Helianthemum 'The Bride'
Helichrysum splendidum
Hesperis matronalis var. *albiflora*
Heuchera 'Green Ivory'

Heuchera 'Palace Purple'
Hosta 'Francee'
Lamium maculatum 'Beacon Silver'
Lavandula angustifolia 'Hidcote'
Ligularia 'The Rocket'
Lychnis coronaria Alba Group
Miscanthus tinctorius 'Variegatus'
Nepeta racemosa 'Walker's Low'
Papaver orientale 'Perry's White'
Polemonium caeruleum var. *album*
Rhodiola rosea
Rosa 'Boule de Neige'
Rosa 'Iceberg'
Rosa 'Margaret Merril'
Rosa 'New Dawn'

Rosa 'Seagull'
Rosa 'Tuscany Superb'
Rosa 'White Meidiland'
Salvia nemorosa 'Ostfriesland'
Salvia nemorosa 'Lubecca'
Salvia officinalis Purpurascens
Salvia pratensis 'Indigo'
Salvia x *sylvestris* 'Blauhügel'
Salvia x *sylvestris* 'Rose Queen'
Santolina chamaecyparissus
Stachys byzantina 'Silver Carpet'
Thalictrum aquilegiifolium
Verbascum chaixii 'Mont Blanc'
Verbascum chaixii 'Pink Domino'
Veronica 'Shirley Blue'
Viola cornuta Alba Group

THE FORGOTTEN PAVILION

It was a massive task to erect the gothic-style arches of Cotswold stone and brick and to lift into place the old iron gate, weighing several tons. But the young designer John Van Hage wanted to create the illusion of coming upon a lost garden; the gateway would provide a glimpse through to the lush overgrown planting of the water garden, with the timber pavilion standing beyond.

The 'forgotten' garden was a common theme in Victorian times, where a corner of a much larger and often formal garden would be given over to the creation of a 'folly', usually with a wilder, abandoned feel to it. This followed a much older tradition of follies and grottoes, the ideas having being brought back by travellers on the grand tour of Europe and manifested in such gardens as Goldney near Bristol and the parks of Wimpole in Cambridgeshire and Hagley Hall in Worcestershire, each with its own 'Gothick ruin'.

Here the gate stands half open, inviting you to venture further. On either side the bold, heart-shaped leaves of the hostas contrast with the feathery flower panicles of the astilbes. Especially striking is the combination of the large, glaucous *Hosta sieboldiana* set against the white plumes of the *Astilbe* 'Deutschland'.

Entering through the gateway we follow the stream as it meanders down the length of the garden over smooth boulders and pebbles. On either side masses of marginal and moisture-loving plants again produce the maximum effect from contrasting foliage, playing within a subtle palette of yellow-greens, variegations and rich greens through to blue-green. A yellow pool of light from the *Carex elata* 'Aurea' is in deep contrast to the dark clumps of hostas and the *Rheum palmatum* 'Astrosanguineum', with its deeply cut leaves and striking plume of coral-pink flowers rising up in early summer. Against the spiky leaves of the grasses and irises, further drifts of the pure white *Astilbe* 'Deutschland' run through the middle distance and lead the eye to the focal point: the open-sided pavilion. Painted a pleasing deep olive, its steep pitched roof of slatted louvres rises up from the planting, bedecked in a climbing wisteria.

An evergreen mix of large shrubs wraps around the edge of the garden, creating deep pools of shade to lose the boundary. Vibrant areas of colour are provided by the scarlet of the rhododendrons, *R.* 'Elizabeth', *R. arboreum*, *R.* 'Mrs G. W. Leak', and the bronze-purple of the *Acer atropurpureum*. A number of large specimen trees, such as the silver birch and evergreen oak, add a feeling of maturity and a timeless sense of stability.

HARPERS & QUEEN
CLASSICAL GARDEN

above: viewed through a row of pleached lime trees, the parterre is a formal, geometric arrangement of gravel paths and triangular beds.

opposite: a mixture of climbing roses, with *Alchemilla mollis* at their feet, and a clump of *Iris sibirica*, are reflected in the still ater of the canal.

The calm classicism of this garden traces its lineage back to the Italian gardens of the High Renaissance, whose architects had absorbed the classical vocabulary of ancient Rome: the belief that beauty lay in formality and symmetry; a sophisticated understanding of proportion; a fondness for sculpture. Few of these gardens survive – they are known mainly from engravings – and the designer, Mark Anthony Walker, describes this as a formal garden based on 17th century French tradition. One of the leading exponents of this tradition was André Le Nôtre, whose brilliant invention, formality and extraordinary precision can be experienced in the gardens of Versailles.

Despite its – at first sight – apparently overwhelming symmetry, Versailles, as originally designed, comprised a complex series of patterned parterres and

bosquets, wooded areas concealed behind tall hedges, forming *salles de verdure*, or green rooms. Each of these 'green rooms' had its own character and held a surprise, such as a statue, fountain or pavilion, to enchant King Louis XIV and his guests. Versailles' gardens in the 17th century were the setting for splendid fêtes, with concerts, dancing and fireworks on a grand scale. The garden we see here follows the tradition of the bosquet, with informal woodland lying beyond the dark, protective, two-metre high clipped yew hedge. Within these green walls we can see how skilfully Mark reinterprets a classical theme to suit a relatively small, modern garden. A key factor is that over the rather hard-edged formal structure he has introduced a soft, informal planting scheme.

The highly architectural, geometric plan has three principle features running parallel across the site. Firstly, the parterre, its pattern of fine gravel pathways intersecting eight tapering segments of massed planting enclosed by clipped box hedging. Four of the beds contain a blend of purple sage and purple alliums, contrasting with the four scented mixes of the silver-leaved *Santolina chamaecyparissus* and the purple-crested flowers of French lavender, *Lavandula stoechas*.

To the right of the parterre, an arched timber arbour painted slate grey is bedecked with hanging racemes of sweetly scented purple wisteria and summer-flowering star jasmine (*Trachelospermum jasminoides*) intermingled with the cool white climbing Iceberg roses and the pale yellow *Rosa* 'Leverkusen'. Running along the base of the arbour on either side of the path is a mixed herbaceous planting including *Alchemilla mollis*, red and white double-flowered *Aquilegia* 'Nora Barlow' and the perennial geraniums 'Johnson's Blue' and *Geranium phaeum* 'Album'.

The full length of the arbour is reflected in the still waters of the narrow canal, another popular feature of classical French gardens. The canal, the third main element of the garden, is an area of calm. Running beside the canal is a grassy path, from which there are enticing glimpses through the arches of the arbour, across the parterre to the abundance of the herbaceous border beyond.

The long herbaceous border to the parterre is planted in a subtle palette of colours and repeats many of the plants used in the arbour. The basic framework is formed of shrubs such as *Viburnum opulus* and *Corylus avellana*. Foxgloves and lupins provide height, and unexpected focal points come in the form of spiral clipped yew bushes. Mark's feeling is that 'You can't have too many vertical herbaceous plants – they give a border perspective and punctuation.'

In the foreground stands a slender line of pleached limes – imported from Italy – their straight trunks and the soft underside of their canopies framing views across the parterre. The pathways are slightly tapering, exaggerating the perspective and drawing the eye to three focal points; two antique stone urns and a towering statue of Mercury, each set within its own niche in the clipped yew hedge.

Not only does this garden encapsulate many of the classical ideals – of balance, harmony, and overall unity and purity of form – it is also a 'classic' according to the dictionary's definition: 'of acknowledged excellence…of lasting interest or significance'. Gardens of this quality, traditional or modern, celebrate the new renaissance in architecture and design, respecting and borrowing from the past in order to create excellence that future generations will applaud and admire.

opposite: the arbour is decked with roses, jasmine and wisteria. At ground level, the planting includes the double red and white flowers of *Aquilegia* 'Nora Barlow, French lavender (*Lavandula stoechas*), *Alchemilla mollis* and the pink flowers of the miniature rose 'Happy Thought'.
below: sculpture has been featured in gardens since Roman times; here, a statue of Mercury forms a focal point in the parterre.

THE DESIGNERS

Geoff Ace has been a lecturer in landscape construction at Merrist Wood College since 1973, and has been Head of the Landscape Department since 1987. He has been involved in most of the gardens created by the College at the Chelsea Flower Show. He emphasizes the need to choose plants appropriate to the conditions and then to use them boldly, and he encourages students to realize the full potential of plants by associating them to create subtle and pleasing effects. Many of his Diploma students have gone on to become well-known garden designers.

*1990 The Mariner's Garden (page 78)
Constructed by students from Merrist Wood College, Worplesdon, Guildford, Surrey GU3 3PE
Tel: +44 (0)1483 884000 Fax: +44 (0)1483 884001

Michael Balston studied architecture at Cambridge, and then requalified as a landscape architect. Since 1983 he has run his own practice in Wiltshire. Balston & Company has designed country gardens, small urban gardens and roof gardens, as well as large-scale private projects in the UK and internationally, often in historically and ecologically sensitive sites. Urban projects include office landscapes and public open spaces in London, Bristol and Paris. The practice is also known for its exhibition work, having won awards not only at Chelsea, but also in Japan, Germany, Belgium and elsewhere. Michael Balston has written a book, *The Well Furnished Garden*, and contributes articles to various magazines and newspapers.
Balston & Company, Long Barn, Patney, Devizes, Wiltshire SN10 3RB
Tel: +44 (0)1380 848181 Fax: +44 (0)1380 848189
Email: admin@balston.co.uk

*1999 Best Garden in Show: The Reflective Garden (page 60)
Sponsor: *Daily Telegraph*
Contractor: Hillier Landscapes, Ampfield House, Ampfield, Romsey, Hampshire SO51 9PA
Tel: +44 (0)1794 368733
Email: hillierlandscapes@bt-internet.com

Mathew Bell see Nuala Hancock

Christopher Bradley-Hole qualified as an architect and worked on a range of prestigious architectural projects before his fascination for plants and gardens led him to study for a post-graduate diploma in the conservation of historic gardens and landscapes. Christopher's designs have ranged from small city courtyards to country acres, in the UK and overseas. His work has been featured widely on television and in the press, and he has contributed a regular design series to the *Daily Telegraph* and *House & Garden*, as well as articles in numerous gardening and design journals. Christopher teaches landscape design to students of the diploma course at the Royal Botanic Gardens, Kew, and is the author of a book on contemporary garden design, *The Minimalist Garden*.
Christopher Bradley-Hole, Studio 10, Sutton Lane North, London W4 4LD
Tel: +44 (020) 8742 1867 Fax: +44 (020) 8995 8005

*1997 Best Garden in Show: The Latin Garden (page 110)
Sponsor: *Daily Telegraph*/American Express
Contractor: Waterers Landscape Ltd, Nursery Court, London Road, Windlesham, Surrey GU20 6LQ
Tel: +44 (0)1344 628081

George Carter studied sculpture at the University of Newcastle upon Tyne. His garden design practice is based in Norfolk. He works on large projects for country houses in Britain and the USA. Recent schemes include: Hayne Manor, Devon; Tilbury Hall, Suffolk; Holkham Hall, Norfolk; Hog Hill Farm; New Hampshire; and Strawberry Ridge, Connecticut. He is also working on projects for the National Trust in Scotland and on several London gardens. George Carter has written a number of books, including *Gardening with Herbs*, *Gardening with Containers*, *Living with Plants* and *London Gardens*. His articles on garden design have appeared in *Country Life*, *The Times*, *Daily Telegraph*, *Country Living*, *Country Homes and Interiors* and many other journals.
George Carter, Silverstone Farm, North Elmham, Norfolk NR20 5EX
Tel: +44 (0)1362 668130 Fax: +44 (0)1362 668141
Email: grcarter@easynet.co.uk

*1999 Sculpture in the Garden (page 118)
Sponsor: Christie, Manson & Woods Ltd
Contractor: Clifton Nurseries, 5a Clifton Villas, London W9 2PH
Tel: +44 (020) 7289 6851

Sir Terence Conran is one of the world's best-known designers. As founder of Habitat, he made good modern design accessible to the general public. He opened The Conran Shop in London in 1973; there are now Conran shops in Europe, the USA and Japan. Equally passionate about food and gardening, he owns a number of restaurants in London – and one in Paris – some of which are supplied with vegetables grown in his own garden at Barton Court in Berkshire. He has written many books on design and in 1998 he collaborated with Dan Pearson (see page 154) to write *The Essential Garden Book*. In 1995, to commemorate the fiftieth anniversary of VE day, Sir Terence collaborated with David Stevens (see page 154) to design a Victory Garden, which won him his first Chelsea gold medal.

*1999 The Chef's Roof Garden (page 86)
Sponsors: *Evening Standard*/Laurent Perrier
Contractor: Michael D Chewter, 21 Lower Green Road, Pembury, near Tunbridge Wells, Kent TN2 4DZ
Tel/fax: +44 (0)1892 822246

Paul Cooper is a former lecturer in Art and Design and a successful sculptor. Since turning to garden design in 1984 he has won a number of medals at Chelsea, and a Best in Show Award. His innovative and sometimes controversial designs, using unconventional materials and theatrical effects, have earned him many commissions: for private gardens, exhibitions and television work. He created a modern garden in the historic setting of Parnham House in Dorset; he made a garden out of car parts for the Ford Motor Company at the Gardeners' World Live show; and he invented an 'Instant Garden' for the BBC series *Gardens by Design*. He is a frequent contributor to television and radio programmes, and he is often asked to lecture at colleges and conferences.
Paul Cooper, Ty Bryn, Old Radnor, Presteigne, Powys LD8 2RN, Wales
Tel/fax: +44 (0)1544 230374

*1992 Best Garden in Show: The Greening of Industry (page 108)
Sponsor: Pan Britannica Industries
Constructed by students from Pershore College of Horticulture, Avonbank, Pershore, WR10 3JP
Tel: +44 (0)1386 552443

Julian Dowle has been a garden designer for 35 years; his work ranges from tiny Japanese courtyards in London to the complete redesign of the grounds of an Oxfordshire manor house, and from landscaping a village in Northern Ireland to the design of a massive cascade for a hotel in Belgium. He is also working on a number of projects in California. His practice covers contemporary and historical gardens, countryside and woodland management, show gardens and exhibitions. Since he first exhibited at Chelsea in 1970 he has won many medals, including nine golds, and a Best in Show Award. Judging and advising at major shows, such as the Ellerslie Flower Show in New Zealand and the Melbourne International Flower and Garden Show in Australia is now an important part of Julian Dowle's work; he is also a sought-after lecturer and broadcaster.
The Julian Dowle Partnership, The Old Malt House, High Street, Newent, Gloucestershire GL18 1AY
Tel: +44 (0)1531 820512 Fax: +44 (0)1531 822421
Email: enquiries@juliandowle.co.uk

*1995 A Japanese Tea Garden (with Koji Ninomiya) (page 56)
Sponsor: Honda UK
Contractor: The Julian Dowle Partnership supported by Action Research
*1994 The Railway Garden (page 134)
Sponsor: *Sunday Express*
Contractor: The Julian Dowle Partnership

Jane Fearnley-Whittingstall's garden designs, books and television appearances have earned her an international reputation. Her work combines a common sense approach to the practical side of gardening with a romantic sense of style and colour in the best English tradition. Her show gardens at Chelsea have won gold medals and prestigious design commissions in the UK and overseas. She has written a number of books, including *Rose Gardens*, *Ivies*, *Peonies – the Imperial Flower* and the best-selling *Gardening Made Easy* and *Garden Plants Made Easy*.
Jane Fearnley-Whittingstall, Merlin Haven House, Wotton-under-Edge, Gloucestershire GL12 7BA
Tel: +44 (0)1453 843228 Fax: +44 (0)1453 521433
E-mail: j_fearnley-whittingstall@msn.com

*1993 A Celebration of Gertrude Jekyll (page 72)
Sponsor: *Country Living* magazine and Kelways Nurseries
Contractor: Andrew Neville

Charles Funke gained his first work experience at the Royal Botanic Gardens, Kew, then went to Bodnant Garden in North Wales. After his military service he joined the well-known horticultural firm Hilliers of Winchester. In 1950, still in his early twenties, he was approached by the BBC and began a weekly national radio broadcast. He has since become a sought-after garden designer, involved in the development of many important estates, with projects extending from London to the Middle East. In 1987, His Highness Shaikh Zayed bin Sultan al-Nahyan, President of the United Arab Emirates, retained Charles Funke to develop the landscape of Tittenhurst Park, near Ascot in Berkshire. He has designed a number of exhibits for His Highness, winning their first Chelsea gold medal in 1998.
Charles Funke Associates, 5 Mill Pool House, Mill Lane, Godalming, Surrey GU7 1EY
Tel: +44 (0)1483 426890

*1999 The Garden of the Book of Gold (page 18)
Sponsor: His Highness Shaikh Zayed bin Sultan Al-Nahyan
Contractor: Landmark Design and Build Ltd, Holloway Hill, Chertsey, Surrey KT16 0AE
Tel: +44 (0)1932 571477

Rupert Golby trained at the Royal Horticultural Society's Gardens at Wisley and the Royal Botanic Gardens, Kew, and gained work experience at Ninfa, near Rome, and in Gloucestershire, working for Rosemary Verey. He began work as a freelance garden designer in 1989. His practice comprises mainly private country gardens in England, although projects have also taken him to Austria and Sweden. In 1999 he won the English Heritage competition to redesign the walled garden at Osborne House on the Isle of Wight. A popular lecturer, he is also a regular contributor to *Country Life* and *Gardens Illustrated*, and is the author of *The Container Garden* and *The Well Planned Garden*.
Rupert Golby, South View, Cross Hill Road, Adderbury West, Banbury, Oxfordshire OX17 3EG
Tel: +44 (0)1295 810320

*1997 *Country Life* Centenary Garden (page 138)
Sponsors: *Country Life* and Hiscox Insurance
Contractor: Pantiles Landscapes Ltd, Almners Road, Lyne, Chertsey, Surrey KT16 0BJ
Tel: +44 (0)1932 872195
*1995 Decorative Kitchen Garden (page 80)
Sponsor: *Country Living* magazine
Contractor: SHAW Landscapes, Station Road, Cramlington, Northumberland NE23 8BJ
Tel: +44 (0)1670 730643

Bunny Guinness runs a landscape architecture business designing a wide range of private gardens and public spaces, from tiny inner city areas to large landscape schemes such as Stapleford Park in Leicestershire and other important estates. She has won five gold medals at Chelsea, for designs that combine a sense of fun and fantasy with superb attention to detail. Bunny Guinness has written two books, *Family Gardens* and *Garden Transformations*, and has contributed to a number of radio and television series, including BBC Radio's *Woman's Hour* and *Gardeners' Question Time*, Channel 4's *Gardeners' Gardens* and Granada's *Better Gardens*.
Bunny Guinness, Sibberton Lodge, Thorhaugh, Peterborough PE8 6NH
Tel: +44 (0)1780 782518

*1999 Portmeirion Garden (page 98)
Contractors: John Courton, Church Farm House, Langtoft, Peterborough PE6 9LP
Tel/fax: +44 (0)1778 343476
Tim Harwood, 1 Irnham Road, Corby Glen, Grantham, Lincs NG33 4NB
Tel: +44 (0)1476 550436
*1998 The Herbalist's Garden (page 8)
Contractor: English Limestone Products, 1a Wellington Lane, Stamford, Lincs PE9 1QB
Tel/fax: +44 (0)1780 764299
*1996 A Touch of Paradise (page 46)
Contractors: John Courton (address as above) and Peter Farrell (formerly Mill Developments), 49 Main Street, Woodnewton, Peterborough PE8 5EB
Tel: +44 (0)1780 470066
*1995 A Writer's Garden (page 7)
Contractor: Mill Developments
*1994 A Children's Garden (page 128)
Contractor: Mill Developments
All sponsored by Wyevale Garden Centres

Marney Hall, ecologist and environmental designer, trained as a scientist, specializing in the management of nature reserves for butterflies. She set up her own company in 1989, but maintains her contacts with butterfly research. She now concentrates on the creation and restoration of natural habitats; her clients have included the Royal Society for the Protection of Birds and the Royal Botanic Gardens at Kew, and she has designed private gardens in the UK, France and the USA. Her expertise in wild flower planting has contributed to a number of gold medal-winning gardens for other designers, besides winning a gold in her own right at Chelsea in 1998. In 1999 her design for an English garden won a Best in Show at the Maymont Flower Festival in Richmond, Virginia. She is a regular contributor to British newspapers and magazines, and has lectured and appeared on radio and television in the UK and the USA.
The Marney Hall Consultancy, Cromwell Cottage, 2 Meadow Lane, St Ives, Cambridge PE17 4JG
Tel/fax: +44 (0)1480 497309

*1998 The Quarryman's Garden (page 122)
Sponsor: Butterfly Conservation
Contractor: The Very Interesting Landscape Company, Cooper House, 2 Michael Road, London SW6 2AD
Tel: +44 (0)1926 313465

Nuala Hancock and **Mathew Bell** met as students at Capel Manor Horticultural College; they work independently, but have also collaborated on joint enterprises.
Nuala Hancock taught French, Art and Design before diversifying into garden design in 1992. Soft Landscape and Design course prize winner at Capel Manor in 1993, she went on, with Mathew Bell, to win a competition to design the Zeneca garden for Chelsea in 1994. Since then, Nuala has worked on many commissions in and around London. She currently writes and lectures in Garden and Planting Design.
Mathew Bell trained in Graphics and had a successful career as a commercial illustrator, which helped greatly in his new vocation as a garden designer. A Member of the Society of Garden Designers, he has created a wide range of gardens for both private and commercial clients.
Nuala Hancock, 6 Chestnut Avenue, London N8 8NY
Tel: +44 (020) 8340 8169
Mathew Bell, 22 Woodside Road, London N22 5HU
Tel: +44 (020) 8881 8329

*1994 The Zeneca Garden (page 42)
Sponsor: Zeneca Ltd (ICI Garden Products)
Constructed by students from Capel Manor Horticultural College, Bullsmoor Lane, Enfield, Middlesex EN1 4RQ
Tel: +44 (020) 8366 4442

Peter Hogan, a trained designer and illustrator, has more than ten years' experience of organizing gardens for Chelsea and other shows. In 1991, on behalf of the *Daily Express*, he commissioned John Van Hage's Forgotton Pavilion (page 146). In 1994 Peter's concept for a disused railway station and garden culminated in the gold medal-winning Railway Garden (page 134). The following year he designed the concept for the Lock-keeper's Garden, working with Frank Hardy and his students at Pershore College. Since 1995 he has worked with various garden designers to produce five medal-winning concepts, including two gold. He has managed a total of 14 gardens at Chelsea, for both the *Daily* and *Sunday Express*, achieving five gold medals.
Peter Hogan, 10 Bryanston Avenue, Whitton, Twickenham, Middlesex TW2 6HP
Tel: +44 (020) 8894 6170

*1995 The Lock-keeper's Garden (with Frank Hardy) (page 26)
Sponsor: *Sunday Express*
Constructed by students from Pershore College of Horticulture, Avonbank, Pershore, WR10 3JP
Tel: +44 (0)1386 552443

Douglas Knight designed his first Chelsea Flower Show garden in 1969. In the ensuing 30 years he has won nine gold medals at Chelsea and his work, specializing in rock and water gardens, has taken him to every part of the British Isles. The location of his business allows him to make regular visits to North Wales, the Lake District and Scotland, where he draws inspiration from the natural waterfalls, streams and mountains. His work has featured in a number of magazines, including *Country Life* and *Ideal Home* in the UK, and *Horticulture* in the United States. In his most exciting challenge to date, he has been commissioned by the Malaysian government to create a series of public gardens on a mountain near the city of Kuala Lumpur.
Douglas G Knight, Freshfield Nurseries, 44 West Lane, Formby, Merseyside L37 7BB
Tel/fax: +44 (0)1704 872880

*1989, 1991, 1995 Rock and Water Gardens (pages 88–90)
Sponsor (1995): Greaves Slate Quarries
Contractor: Douglas G Knight

Fiona Lawrenson trained as a horticulturist at Merrist Wood College, and gained work experience at the Royal Horticultural Society garden at Wisley before establishing her own landscape garden business, Floribunda, in 1991. She started exhibiting in 1994, and in 1996, aged 27, she won a gold medal at Chelsea; she went on to win a second gold medal the following year. Her career in television began in 1996 with the presentation of a weekly programme, *Gardening with Fiona Lawrenson*, broadcast by British Sky Broadcasting. In 1998 she became a presenter of

Real Gardens for Channel 4. Her company, now renamed, specializes in large garden projects and the restoration of established gardens.
Fiona Lawrenson Ltd, Thursley Lodge, Farnham Lane, Haslemere, Surrey GU27 1HA
Tel/fax: +44 (0)1428 651776

*1997 A Garden in Provence (page 104)
*1996 New England Cottage (page 14)
Sponsor: British Sky Broadcasting
Contractor: Landmark Design and Build Ltd, Holloway Hill, Chertsey, Surrey KT16 0AE
Tel: +44 (0)1932 571477

Arabella Lennox-Boyd left her native Rome to settle in England, and has been a landscape designer for the past 20 years. Her commissions have ranged from small town gardens and roof gardens to large historical country landscapes, including gardens for the National Trust, and projects in France, Germany, Belgium, Italy, Spain, Mexico, Barbados, Canada and the USA. She has designed four gold-medal-winning gardens for Chelsea, including a Best in Show Award in 1998. She lectures in the UK and overseas, and is a member of the Historic Parks and Gardens Panel of English Heritage. She has written two books: *Traditional English Gardens* and *Private Gardens of London*.
Arabella Lennox-Boyd, 45 Moreton Street, London SW1V 2NY
Tel: +44 (020) 7931 9995 Fax: +44 (020) 7821 6585
Email: office@alboffice.edi.co.uk

*1995 The National Trust Centenary Garden (page 28)
Contractor: Michael D Chewter, 21 Lower Green Road, Pembury, near Tunbridge Wells, Kent TN2 4DZ
Tel/fax: +44 (0)1892 822246
*1993 A Romantic Woodland Garden (page 118)
Contractor: Townscapes, 30a Pimlico Road, London SW1W 8LJ
Tel: +44 (020) 7730 4061 Fax: +44 (020) 7730 0480

*1990 The English Country Garden (page 142)
Contractor: Pathfinder Gardening
All sponsored by the *Daily Telegraph*.

John Moreland, 24 Alma Terrace, Penzance, Cornwall TR18 2BY
Tel: +44 (0)1736 367525

Dan Pearson trained at the Royal Horticultural Society's gardens at Wisley, at Merrist Wood College and at the Royal Botanic Gardens at Kew and won scholarships to Spain, India and Israel. As a garden designer and consultant, he has worked in the UK, France and Italy, and his exhibition work has won a gold and several other medals at Chelsea. His garden designs have featured in numerous magazines, including *Gardens Illustrated* and *Elle Decoration*, and on

BBC 2's *Gardeners' World* and *The Front Garden*. He was the presenter and designer of two series of *Garden Doctors* for Channel 4; he has also presented his own series, *Dan Pearson: Routes Around the World*. Since 1994 he has written a weekly column for *The Sunday Times*, and he is co-author, with Sir Terence Conran, of *The Essential Garden Book*.
Dan Pearson, 80c Battersea Rise, London SW11 1EH
Tel/fax: +44 (020) 7924 2518

*1996 A London Roof Garden (page 38)
Sponsor: *Evening Standard ES* magazine
Contractor: Daniel Pearson and Yeo Associates

Roger Platts trained in horticulture, specializing in nursery production, then worked in nurseries in the UK and Denmark before setting up his own garden design business in 1989. Roger has created three Chelsea show gardens, two of which won gold medals. In 1996 he purchased a nursery at Edenbridge in Kent, which required some restoration. The nursery aims to be a garden full of ideas, using planting and features taken from his Chelsea gardens, and to provide a wide range of interesting plants, including unusual shrubs and perennials, backed up with helpful advice. Roger now has a team of experienced horticulturalists producing plants, assisting with design and creating gardens throughout the UK.
Roger Platts, Stick Hill, Edenbridge, Kent TN8 5NH
Tel: +44 (0)1732 863318

*1997 The Spout Garden (page 92)
Contractor: Roger Platts Garden Design and Nurseries and Jupp & Sons

David Stevens started his horticultural career more than 30 years ago, combining practical work with formal training in landscape architecture. He formed his own practice in 1972, becoming landscape consultant to *Homes & Gardens* magazine and creating gardens for clients all over Europe, in America, the West Indies and the Middle East. He built his first Chelsea Flower Show garden in 1972, and went on to win 26 awards, including 11 gold medals, with three Best in Show Awards. He is in great demand internationally as a consultant and lecturer, and is Professor of Garden Design at Middlesex University. In 1997 he launched an international correspondence course in Garden Design. David Stevens is the author of 17 books, has made numerous radio broadcasts and has scripted and presented many television programmes and series, including *Gardens by Design* and *Gardenwise* for the BBC.
David Stevens International, Corner Cottage, Thornton, Buckinghamshire MK17 0HE
Tel/fax: +44 (0)1280 821097
E-mail: gardens@david-stevens.co.uk

*1990 A Garden for Roses (page 34)
*1992 Rockscape (page 91)
Contractor: Class Gardens, 2 Ponsbourne Park,
Newgate Street Village, Hertfordshire SG13 8QU
Tel: +44 (0)1707 874793
Both sponsored by B & Q plc

Tom Stuart-Smith has been a practising landscape architect since 1984; much of his work has been associated with historic gardens. Early in his career he created the garden at Plumpton Place, Sussex – a moated mediaeval house reconstructed by Sir Edwin Lutyens. Among other notable projects, he has designed a new park at Wormsley, Oxfordshire; the Chancery Garden at the British Embassy, Paris; the regeneration of an important garden in Jersey; a genetics research campus for the Wellcome Trust near Cambridge; and work for the Royal Horticultural Society at Rosemoor in Devon. His own garden in Hertfordshire has featured in a number of publications, including *House & Garden* and the Saturday *Times* magazine, and has been shown on BBC *Gardeners' World*. He has now joined forces with Todd Longstaffe-Gowan and Patrick James to form the Landscape Agency, a consultancy offering design, conservation and practical management services.
The Landscape Agency, Kirkman House,
12–14 Whitfield Street, London W1P 5RD
Tel: +44 (020) 7631 3185 Fax: +44 (020) 7631 3186
E-mail: tom@landscapeagency.co.uk

*1998 Le Bosquet de Chanel (page 74)
Sponsor: Chanel
Contractor: Waterers Landscape Ltd, Nursery
Court, London Road, Windlesham, Surrey
GU20 6LQ
Tel: +44 (0)1344 628081

Julie Toll trained in landscape and garden design, and her work has taken her throughout Europe, the USA and the West Indies. Her first Chelsea Flower Show garden in 1990 was rewarded with a gold medal; she has gone on to win a further four gold medals at Chelsea, and a Best in Show Award. She has created a wide range of gardens, from roof terraces to country estates and golf courses, and has developed her particular talent for wild flower and wildlife gardens. Julie Toll was a co-presenter of the BBC 2 series *Gardens by Design*, and is a popular lecturer. Her first book, *The Small Garden*, was published by the Royal Horticultural Society.
Julie Toll Landscape & Garden Design, 44 Sefton
Road, Stevenage, Hertfordshire SG1 5RJ
Tel: +44 (0)1438 318494 Fax: +44 (0)1438 747518
E-mail: Julie.Toll@btinternet.com

*1996 A Forest Garden (page 66)
Sponsor: Pro-Carton
Contractor: Bramble Garden Landscapes, Tree
Farm, Carneles Green, Broxbourne, Hertfordshire
EN10 6PW
Tel: +44 (0)1992 469825

Xa Tollemache studied History of Art at the Sorbonne in Paris. Always a keen gardener, she acquired a practical training with Roy Balaam, head gardener at Helmingham Hall, her husband's family home for 500 years. The garden they developed was considered by Rosemary Verey to be one of the most outstanding in the country; it has been featured in numerous television programmes, books and magazine articles. Xa Tollemache became a professional garden designer in 1995; she was immediately commissioned by Lord and Lady Astor to design a planting scheme at Ginge Manor, Oxfordshire. The following year the Astors asked her to create a new Terrace Garden at Castle Heaton, Northumberland, which was featured in *House & Garden* magazine. Working in the UK, France and the USA, she has since designed a wide range of gardens, both formal and informal.
Xa Tollemache, Helmingham Hall, Stowmarket,
Suffolk IP14 6EF
Tel: +44 (0)1473 890799 Fax: +44 (0)1473 890776
E-mail: xatollemache@aol.com

*1997 Classical Calm with a Touch of Tomorow
(page 50)
Sponsor: *Evening Standard*
Contractor: Michael D Chewter, 21 Lower Green
Road, Pembury, near Tunbridge Wells, Kent
TN2 4DZ
Tel/fax: +44 (0)1892 822246

John Van Hage underwent extensive horticultural training and studied landscape design under the internationally renowned garden designer John Brookes. Between studies he worked in the family business, Van Hage Garden Co., eventually becoming a director of the company. He has since set up his own company, Van Hage Design Co.; his clients include showbusiness personalities and companies such as Pan Britannica Industries. He first exhibited at Chelsea Flower Show in 1990; the following year, aged 25, he became the youngest designer ever to win a Gold Medal at the Show. He has recently been involved in writing and producing a CD-ROM, *The Home Garden Planner*, setting up a television production company, Palimpsest Productions, and setting up a website, www.horticom.co.uk.
Van Hage Design Co., 65 Ennismore Gardens,
London SW7 1NH
Tel: +44 (020) 7584 6254 Fax: +44 (020) 7823 8416

*1996 A Japanese Artist's Garden (page 102)
Sponsor: Bio & Hillhut
Contractor: James Steele-Sargent, 8 Willow Walk,
Petworth, Sussex GU28 0EY
Tel: +44 (0)1798 343960
*1991 Best Garden in Show: The Forgotten Pavilion
(page 146)
Sponsor: Express Newspapers
Contractor: Van Hage Garden Company, Pepper
Hill, Great Amwell, Hertfordshire SG12 9RP
Tel: +44 (0)1920 870811

Mark Anthony Walker studied landscape architecture and design to post-graduate level. He then gained extensive experience of working with architects and interior designers as well as a landscape design company, developing both contemporary and historic landscapes before setting up his own practice in 1996. His commercial work, combined with his success at Chelsea – he has won four gold medals and a Best in Show – established his international reputation, and his client base is wide-ranging in the UK, Europe and the Middle East. Projects include: a large country estate and office campus development in Micklenburg, near Rostock in eastern Germany; urban design for new artists' studios in London, and a wide variety of private gardens and landscape design projects in England and Italy.
Mark Anthony Walker, 4 The Cottages, Sergehill
Lane, Bedmond, Hertfordshire WD5 0RZ
Tel/fax: +44 (0)1923 266303
E-mail: mark.a.walker@btinternet.com

*1998 A Water Meadow Garden (page 126)
Contractor: Park Garden Services, 6 Shepherds
Rise, Vernham Dean, Andover, Hants SP11 0HD
Tel/fax: +44 (0)1264 737296
*1995 The Olive Grove (page 20)
*1994 Classical Garden (page 148)
Both sponsored by Cartier/*Harpers & Queen*
Contractor for both gardens: Clifton Nurseries,
5a Clifton Villas, London W9 2PH
Tel: +44 (020) 7289 6851

Robin Williams has, over the past 40 years, designed more than 1,200 gardens and has taught and lectured on garden design in Europe, Japan and the USA. He is a past Chairman of the Society of Garden Designers (UK) and a member of the Association of Professional Landscape Designers (USA), who in 1998 honoured his outstanding contribution to the landscape profession with a surprise award at their conference in New Orleans. He has contributed to and written a number of books, including *The Garden Designer* and *Garden Planning (*in the *RHS Encyclopaedia of Practical Gardening* series), and has written and illustrated articles for *Popular Gardening* and other publications. He has also acted as consultant and designer to several BBC television series, including *Gardeners' World*. He runs his international landscape design consultancy practice in partnership with his son Robin Templar Williams, also an award-winning garden designer.
Robin Williams & Associates, Rowan House,
Winterton Drive, Speen, Newbury, Berkshire
RG14 1UD
Tel: +44 (0)1635 32910 Fax: +44 (0)1635 36625
E-mail: robin@robinwilliams.co.uk

*1990 A Garden of Golden Memories (page 62)
Sponsor: Enterprise Oil plc
Contractor: Allseasons Landscapes, Prospect House,
The Green, Ninfield, Battle, East Sussex TN33 9JE
Tel: +44 (0)1424 893222

INDEX

Romantic Woodland Garden 116-17
roof gardens 38-41, 86-7
Rosa (roses) 14, 16-17, *30*, 31, 34-7, *51*, 52, *80*, *141*, *150*
   R. 'Albertine' 92, *140*
   R. 'Ballerina' *34*
   R. 'Buff Beauty' 17, 64
   R. 'Emily Gray' 72
   R. 'Félicité Perpétue' 97
   R. filipes 'Kiftsgate' 97, *100*
   R. gallica 'Versicolor' *55*, 84
   R. glauca 54, 139
   R. 'Goldfinch' *80*
   R. 'Happy Thought' *150*
   R. 'Iceberg' *30*, *36*, 145, 151
   R. 'Korresia' *34*
   R. 'Leverkusen' 151
   R. 'Madame Grégoire Staechelin' 82
   R. 'Margaret Merril' 145
   R. 'Marjorie Fair' *34*, *36*
   R. mundi see *R. gallica* 'Versicolor'
   R. 'New Dawn' 37, 97
   R. 'Parkdirektor Riggers' *116*
   R. 'Portmeirion' 98
   R. 'Pretty Polly' *35*
   R. 'Rambling Rector' 72, *93*, 97
   R. 'Reine Victoria' 97
   R. 'Roseraie de l'Haÿ' 17
   R. 'Sander's White Rambler' 82
   R. 'Seagull' 64, 98, *100*, *117*
   R. 'Spirit of Youth' 34, 36
   R. 'Tuscany Superb' *83*, 145
   R. 'Tynwald' 64
   R. 'White Meidiland' *30*
Rosmarinus officinalis (rosemary) 107, 111, 121
Rubus 'Parsley Leaved' 84

Salix alba 126
   S.a. 'Vitellina' 130
   S. caladendron 126
   S. elaeagnos 130
   S. exigua 44
   S. purpurea 'Nancy Saunders' 139
Salvia 82, 111
   S. x *superba* 96
   S. x *sylvestris* 'Mainacht' *55*, 95
   S. verticillata 'Purple Rain' 95
Sambucus nigra 'Guincho Purple' 54
Santolina 9, 31, *106*
   S. chamaecyparissus 40, 151
   S.c. 'Lambrook Silver' *119*, 121
   S. rosmarinifolia 9

sculpture garden 118-21
Sempervivum tectorum 82
Senecio cineraria 121
Sexton, Jack 91
Sickert, Walter 140-1
Simmons, Neil 121
Simpson, John 105, 140
Sisyrinchium striatum 138
   S.s. 'Aunt May' 95, *95*
Society of Apothecaries 10
Solanum crispum 97
Soldani Benzi, Massimiliano 77
Spiraea 54
   S. x *vanhouttei* 117
Spout Garden 92-7
Stachys 114
   S. byzantina 121
Stackallan 77
Stevens, David 34-6, 91, 154
Stowe 77
Stuart-Smith, Tom 74, 155
Stumm, Johannes von 139-40
succulents 133
Sunday Express 27
Syringa vulgaris 'Madame Lemoine' 77

Thalictrum 114
   T. aquilegiifolium 145
Thymus 9, 111
   T. 'Bertram Anderson' 40
   T. serpyllum minimus 10
   T. 'Silver Posie' 40, 95
Tiarella cordifolia 71
Till, Rupert 141
Toll, Julie 66-70, 155
Tollemache, Xa 50-5, 155
topiary 121
Trachelospermum jasminoides 151
Trachycarpus fortunei 18, 47
Tradescantia x *andersoniana* 70
Trollius 72
   T. chinensis 'Golden Queen' *88*
   T. europaeus 130
trompe l'oeil 9, *11*, 105, 140
Tropaeolum majus 48
Tsuga heterophylla 17
tulips 9, *13*
Typha maxima 97
   T. minima 129

Vaccinium corymbosum 17
Van Hage, John 102-3, 146, 155
vegetables 80-4, *80-5*, 86-7, *87*, 130, *132*

Verbascum *51*, *55*, 84, 114
   V. 'Arctic Summer' *110-11*
   V. bombyciferum 130
   V.b. 'Mont Blanc' 77
   V. 'Gainsborough' 64, *66*, *69*
   V. 'Helen Johnson' 40, *106*, 107
Veronica gentianoides 68
   V.g. 'Tissington White' *15*, *106*
Versailles 148-51
Viburnum 28, 54, 60
   V. opulus *8*, *16*, 97, 117, 151
   V. plicatum 'Mariesii' 97
   V. sargentii 'Onondaga' 77
Viola 15
   V. 'Scarlet' *32*
   V. tricolor *124*
Virgil *4*, 110-15
Vitis 'Brant' *80*, 82

Walker, Mark Anthony 20-4, 126, 148-51, 155
Water Meadow Garden 126-7
waterfalls 88-91
West, Gilbert 77
Western hemlock 17, *17*
Wharton, Robert 34
Whichford Pottery 98
wild flowers 141
wild gardens 122-5
Williams, David 125
Williams, Robin 62-4, 155
Williams-Ellis, Sir Clough 98, *101*
Wimpole 146
Wisteria 28, 146, *150*, 151
   W. sinensis 'Alba' 24, *25*
woodland gardens 116-17
Writer's Garden *7*

Xanthorrhoea australis 47
Xanthosoma violaceum 49

yew 30, *30*, 31, *100*, 121, 142, *142*, 143, 145, 151
Yucca 60
   Y. elephantipes 49

Zantedeschia aethiopica 126
   Z.a. 'Crowborough' 53, 98, *116*
   Z. elliottiana 49
Zayed bin Sultan Al-Nahyan, Shaikh 18
Zeneca Garden 42-5

ACKNOWLEDGMENTS

PICTURE CREDITS

The author and publishers would like to thank the photographers whose pictures appear on these pages; their co-operation has been invaluable.

Malcolm Birkitt: 56
John Glover: 4, 8 (bottom), 13, 17, 39, 41, 44 (bottom), 45, 48, 58, 75, 98, 102, 115 (both), 122 (top), 123, 126, 140, 146, 150
Barry Gould: 108, 109
Jerry Harpur: 19, 26, 27, 32, 35, 36, 60, 64, 89, 90, 91, 95, 116, 117, 119, 128, 129, 132, 135, 136, 138, 142, 144, 145
Marcus Harpur: 8 (top), 12, 47, 50, 87, 99, 103, 105, 107 (top), 127, 139, 141 (top)
Derek Harris: 100, 101, 122 (bottom), 124
Andrew Lawson: 14, 28, 29, 33, 38, 42, 44 (top), 46, 62, 65, 66, 78, 80, 81, 86, 114, 118, 120, 137, 147
Marianne Majerus: 10, 55, 77, 93, 104
John Moreland: 79
National Magazines/Country Living (Clive Boursnell) 72, 73
National Magazines/Harpers & Queen (Jonathan Pilkington) 22, 148, 149
Clive Nichols: 11, 20, 24 (both), 30, 59, 61, 70, 84, 85, 88, 97, 121, 141 (bottom), 151
Jonathan Pilkington/The Interior Archive: 21, 25
Derek St Romaine: 3, 9, 15, 16, 49, 51, 52, 54 (both), 57, 67, 68, 69, 71, 74, 76, 83, 92, 96, 106, 107 (bottom), 110-111
David Stevens: 34
Juliette Wade: 7
Steven Wooster/Garden Picture Library: 43
Steven Wooster: 131, 133

Illustrations by Karl Pitwon
Illustration on page 101 reproduced by kind permission of Robin Llywelyn

AUTHOR'S ACKNOWLEDGMENTS

I wish to warmly thank everyone who has helped and encouraged me with this book since its conception some five years ago: everyone at Cassell – with a special thanks to Maggie Ramsay, whose dedication and time spent were beyond the normal call of duty; the featured garden designers, whose co-operation has been very much appreciated; all the photographers, without whose talent this book would not have been possible; and my agent, Fiona Lindsay, who made it happen.

I particularly wish to thank my colleague and friend of some…well, never mind how many…years, David Stevens, who first 'turned me on' to garden design and introduced me to the fun and games of creating show gardens at Chelsea. Thanks also to another dear friend and colleague from those early college days, Arabella Lennox-Boyd, whose phone call in 1989 set us both on a path to three Gold Medals and then a Gold and Best in Show; it was this experience that was the true inspiration for this book. Finally, a very special thank you to dear friends Barbara and Alan Lumsden, whose support and encouragement and encyclopaedic knowledge – of plants and 'all things' respectively – has been of such help.

PUBLISHER'S NOTE

Every effort has been made to check the accuracy of plant names. However, botanical and taxonomic nomenclature is subject to revision by the Royal Horticultural Society, and some well-known plant names have changed since the gardens were designed. Additionally, the lists drawn up by the garden designers are subject to change, depending on what is available and in good condition at the time of construction of the show garden, and last-minute changes may not always be noted. The plant lists in this book suggest typical planting to achieve the effects of the gold medal-winning gardens.